BITE SIZE ADVICE 2
The Lesson Continues...

Bite Size Advice 2

The Lesson Continues ... A Further Guide to Political, Economic, Social and Technological Issues

Paul J. Thomas

Copyright 2016 Paul J. Thomas

In accordance with the U.S. Copyright Act of 1976, and the Australian Copyright Act of 1968, the scanning, uploading and electronic sharing of any part of this book without the permission of the publisher constitutes unlawful piracy and theft of the author's intellectual property. If you would like to use material from the book (other than for review purposes), prior written permission must be obtained by contacting the publisher at info@goko.com.au

GOKO Management and Publishing
PO Box 7109
McMahons Point 2060
Sydney, Australia
First Edition 2016

Library of Congress Cataloging-in-Publication Data

Thomas, Paul J.
    Bite Size Advice 2: The Lesson Continues ... A Further Guide to Political, Economic, Social and Technological Issues

    p. cm.
    ISBN: 978-1-61339-870-8
    LCCN: 2016903977
        BUSINESS & ECONOMICS/General
        BUSINESS & ECONOMICS/Government & Business
        BUSINESS & ECONOMICS/Education

Every attempt has been made to trace accurate ownership of copyrighted material in this book. Errors and omissions will be corrected in subsequent editions, provided that notification is sent to the publisher.

The views expressed in this publication are those of the author and not necessarily those of Gateway Credit Union Ltd.

This is for you, Beverley. Thanks for being a great wife and for allowing me to dedicate this book to you.
You deserve to be between the covers.

ALSO BY PAUL J. THOMAS

Bite Size Advice: A definitive guide to political, economic, social and technological issues (Vol. 1)

Preface

This second volume of *Bite Size Advice* is, like the first volume, a collection of blog posts. When the first volume was published in June 2015, the decision was made to include only 100 of a potential 300 posts. Limiting the number of posts to be printed was seen as essential to achieve the desired book length - that of a small novel.

This companion volume, *Bite Size Advice 2*, contains an additional 100 blog posts. These posts were either excluded from the first volume or written since its publication. In presenting these supplementary posts, this present volume carries forward the structure of the first volume. To this end, the posts coalesce around the same four thematic chapters found in volume one.

Additionally, this second volume is augmented with a bonus fifth chapter containing Christmas parodies. My final blog post each calendar year is a light-hearted review of the preceding 12 months set to the rhythm and rhyme of *The Night Before Christmas*. It was decided not to include the parodies in volume one, but I am delighted to present them here for your enjoyment.

While splitting the blog posts has resulted in two publications, they are independent works. This book is not a sequel but a self-contained second instalment in a two-volume set. *Bite Size Advice 2* can be read without the need to read *Bite Size Advice (1)*. No prior knowledge of the contents of volume one is required or presupposed.

Given this, reprinted on the succeeding pages are the Foreword, Introduction and Afterword from volume one. This was deemed necessary to provide first time readers of the *Bite Size Advice* series with an understanding of the background to the blog and how the posts came to be published in book format in the first place.

The reader familiar with the original *Bite Size Advice* will find some subject overlap in these pages. The 100 posts that comprise this book represent new content and are published here for the very first time. In some cases, however, the topics covered are similar to those found in the first volume, albeit they are tackled from a different angle with new lines of thought.

What is contained in this volume is not the result of breakthrough thinking in an academic sense. This is not a work of original scholarship but a critical synthesis of prevailing opinions and ideas brought together to produce fresh perspectives. I offer no discoveries that will contribute to the advancement of human knowledge, only thoughtful consideration and analysis of contemporary issues.

When I started my blogging career, I was strongly advised to keep my posts short - no more than 350 words. I reluctantly kept to that word-count threshold for about three years but ultimately found it too restrictive. Over recent years, my posts have averaged around 700 words making them more content rich. This work contains a mix of short and long form blog posts giving the reader the opportunity to assess first-hand if size does matter.

PREFACE

Every author's work is unique and *Bite Size Advice* does not fit neatly into one clearly defined literary genre. My intended audience, therefore, remains broad and diverse. This volume is a business book, an educational book and a general knowledge book. It is for anyone who wants to understand how the world around us works.

I remarked in the introduction to volume one that "never in my wildest dreams" did I think my blog posts would one day be turned into a book. I now express even greater amazement that another compendium of posts is being released and that its appearance has occurred so soon. I am gratified and humbled at the acceptance of volume one and hope that this tome also succeeds in finding an appreciative audience.

My purpose will be fulfilled if readers find this book both informative and enjoyable. I am reminded of the words of American novelist, Nathaniel Hawthorne, who said that "easy reading is damn hard writing". I know how difficult it is to write prose that flows effortlessly. While I am unable to guarantee that my words will jump off the page, I do hope they are enticing.

Producing a book is never a solo endeavour. I cannot, therefore, conclude this preface without articulating my sincere appreciation to the four women who helped me create what I hope is another coherent text. These women were my support team in giving life to volume one and they have repeated their unstinting efforts to produce this second volume.

First and foremost, I wish to voice my deep thanks to my PA, Marisa Dul. She did not flinch when I told her there would be another book to test her inexhaustible supply of patience. Marisa graciously accepted the constant fine-tuning of the manuscript and the never-ending changes. She is like family and has been an untiring supporter and loyal colleague for over a decade.

Someone else who did not run away when I suggested we do it all again was my publisher, Katherine Owen. Shaping a book out of 100 blog posts is no easy task and Katherine was again up for the challenge. We got on even better the second time around. Perhaps that's because I told Katherine that the author always has the final say, so she readily nurtured my ideas!

Standing in the shadows throughout this book's gestation was Gateway Credit Union's Chairman, Catherine Hallinan. Catherine does not seek the limelight but stays discretely in the background offering behind-the-scenes guidance. She is an invaluable sounding board who provides clear insights as a mentor, colleague and friend.

Finally, I extend my heartfelt gratitude to my wife, Beverley Thomas. In my writing endeavours, she is my biggest fan to the point of her own sacrifice. Beverley happily allows me to write my weekly posts on Saturday afternoons even though this impacts our time together. We are great collaborators and to her I truly owe an unrepayable debt.

Notwithstanding the wonderful assistance I have received to bring this book to fruition, any errors or omissions are definitely my own. For these and any other failings in my writing, I apologise.

Paul J. Thomas
Sydney, June 2016

This book contains a cross-section of blog posts organised thematically into five chapters. Each chapter contains posts covering a common theme. By arranging the posts into discrete subject areas, the reader is able to find all the content about a specific topic in one chapter, making browsing by interest much easier. Note that the chapters can be read in any order and that each chapter begins with a brief introduction. Please also note that the posts contained in each chapter are not presented in chronological order. Given this, each post ends with a footnote showing the original publishing date to provide a timestamp and historic context.

Contents

	Preface	*ix*
	Foreword	*xvii*
	Introduction	*xxi*
01	Political Influences	1
02	Economic Trends	37
03	Social Changes	131
04	Technological Advances	207
05	Christmas Parodies	247
	Afterword	*263*
	Resource List	*267*
	About the Author	*279*

Foreword

It is estimated that there are over 150 million blogs on the Internet and the number continues to rise. The blogosphere has rapidly become a big and busy world yet is still relatively new. The first blog was written by a college student in 1994 and a decade later the word blog was declared word of the year by Merriam-Webster.

While there are many blogs, not all are created equal. One which stands out from the crowd is a thought-provoking and eclectic blog written by Paul Thomas. Paul is the Chief Executive Officer of Gateway Credit Union in Sydney. Gateway was a relatively early adopter of blogging and maintains one of Australia's leading business blogs.

Australian companies remain cautious about embracing social media tools like blogs. In contrast, Paul has been putting a human face to Gateway via his CEO Blog since March 2008. Paul is living proof that blogging is no longer the sole realm of geeks and believes that corporations without blogs are faceless entities.

This book is a compelling collection of some of Paul's blog posts - 100 to be exact. His weekly posts are a combination of economic commentary, thought leadership and financial hints. What ties these seemingly disparate categories together is that they are all written through the prism of a banking and financial services lens.

Of course, you can't talk about banking without talking about money, since the two are so intertwined. Paul has written about the history of money, the future of money and the creation of money. He has also published posts on money etiquette, money disorders and money management.

Money comes in many forms and Paul has explained the workings of fiat money, credit money and virtual money. He has also outlined how money affects Wall Street and Main Street and how money and debt are two sides of the same coin. He has described the operation of monetary policy and the use of quantitative easing.

As a business blogger, Paul is not an uncritical apologist for free markets because no economic or political system built by humans is perfect. But as an economic rationalist, Paul is proud to nail his colours to the mast and declare he remains a proud supporter of open markets - even with their imperfections.

To this end, he has published blogs in defence of globalisation, deficits and bailouts. He has stood up for free enterprise and capitalism while underscoring the need for greater ethics and accountability in banking and highlighting the pitfalls of over-regulation.

Along the way, he has pointed out the dangers of excessive leverage, the importance of savings and the need to educate our children and young adults in money matters. From Islamic banking to fractional reserve banking, Paul educates and informs in an easy-to-understand and entertaining way.

The Global Financial Crisis provided Paul with a rich source of developing and unfolding events to comment upon. He explained both the cause of and response to the crisis. The crisis exposed the greedy and destructive side of human nature at both an institutional and individual level.

Paul has a deep understanding of the human condition and is passionate about people and human behaviour. That passion finds expression in the humanistic narrative thread that weaves seamlessly through his blog. Economics is the study of human behaviour as it applies to money and Paul's musings on money and life have touched a chord with a growing readership.

This book's strength lies in its accessibility. Each blog post is succinct and can therefore be digested quickly and easily. This compendium, then, is perfect for the time-starved reader and for those with short attention spans since all posts are concise yet informative.

By avoiding excessive jargon and clearly explaining key concepts, *Bite Size Advice* demystifies key issues which impact our day-to-day lives. It fills a gap in the literature on contemporary political, economic, social and technological issues in a user-friendly way.

You will discover that Paul is a storyteller who eases readers into complex topics while offering authoritative insights and opinions. I am an avid reader of Gateway's CEO Blog which Paul religiously updates every Monday morning to keep it fresh and relevant.

Under Paul's leadership, Gateway has grown from an institution with little brand recognition to a respected name in the financial services sector. He is passionate about Gateway's *"people helping people"* philosophy and believes that credit unions must constantly change while forever staying the same.

Paul has had a long and successful career in financial

services. He is a resourceful and strategic CEO who has forged a reputation as a thought leader. An accomplished public speaker and writer, Paul's credentials include an MBA and a Diploma in Financial Services.

In the pages that follow, you will find an informative collection of Paul's blog posts. Persuasive in argument and wide in sweep, they offer a fascinating window into many of the contemporary political, economic, social and technological issues facing society. I hope you enjoy reading them as much as I did.

C.M. Hallinan
Chairman
Gateway Credit Union Ltd
Sydney, June 2015

Introduction

Never in my wildest dreams did I think my blog posts would one day be turned into a book. When I took my first uncertain steps as a rookie blogger in March 2008, I thought I would quickly run out of steam. Seven years later I can safely say my concern was unfounded.

I took to blogging like a duck to water and have never missed a weekly posting, even though I still lose sleep worrying about the content of next week's blog! I find blogging extremely rewarding as it enables me to show a more human side to banking and finance.

From the outset, I have used my blog to offer what I hope have been enlightening insights into the often misunderstood world of banking and finance. I have tried to shine an instructive light on the inner workings of a sector that touches the daily lives and wallets of billions of people around the world.

Whether it's taking out a mortgage to buy a home, obtaining capital to start a business, transferring money to electronically pay bills, putting savings away to fund one's retirement or insuring your life and personal possessions, the financial services industry plays a key role.

Indeed, the financial services industry is the hub of an

economy, facilitating the productive flow of funds between sectors, companies and individuals. The banking industry plays a critical role in fuelling economic growth by providing credit to households, businesses and governments.

Money, of course, is a central component of our lives and influences practically every decision that we make. We need money to pay for our basic needs (food, clothing and shelter) and to finance our non-essential wants (exotic holidays, luxury cars and designer goods).

Some people are defined by money, others see money as merely a means to an end while others still have very little money. This economic inequality has driven me to opine on the extremes of wealth and poverty, highlighting the gap between the richest and poorest in society.

Humans love to debate and argue their point. Some high profile debates I have weighed into include the population debate, the climate debate, the welfare debate and the privatisation debate. On a lighter note, I also debated the merits of maintaining a corporate wardrobe.

Maintaining a corporate blog has clearly enabled me to share my ideas and opinions on a range of political, economic, social and technological topics. What I have learned along the way is that you have to distil a lot of information into a coherent and cohesive argument or summary.

If the truth be known, I was initially a very reluctant blogger and was dragged into blogging by a colleague who argued that it would be good for Gateway and for me. I find it hard to imagine my professional life without blogging - it's become part and parcel of my working week.

The golden rule of blogging is that you have to be authentic, so my blog is an online extension of my personality. My overarching aim is to be an honest and transparent blogger who tries to inform and debate in an entertaining way.

In March 2013 I celebrated my fifth anniversary as a blogger which caused me to look at the blog with fresh eyes. What struck me is that my blog, unlike most others, did not have a name. Choosing a personal blog title is something I overlooked when my blog was launched.

I was told that the best blog titles are short, compelling and easy to find in search results. So, I chose to name my blog, *Doubting Thomas*. The term Doubting Thomas can be viewed in a negative or positive light depending on whether you are a destructive cynic or a constructive sceptic and I am the latter.

Cynicism is a mind-set of automatic doubt whereas scepticism employs critical thinking to determine validity. The word sceptic is from the Greek word *skeptikos* which means to inquire or find out. It is said that scepticism (factual analysis) is the best way of seeking the truth.

The French mathematician, scientist and philosopher, René Descartes (1596-1650), insisted on thinking for himself rather than simply accepting what he had been taught. He resolved to hold nothing true until he could be absolutely certain of it.

Descartes eventually discovered that the one thing he could never doubt was the fact that he himself existed, since the very act of doubting required a doubter. He expressed this conclusion in the now famous Latin phrase *"Cogito, ergo sum"* - I think, therefore I am. To paraphrase Descartes - I think, therefore I blog.

Finally, please note that each blog post was originally written to be read independently of the rest. Given this fact, some repetition and overlap occurs when stand-alone posts covering the same topic - albeit from different angles - are reproduced together in this one book.

01 Political Influences

▪ ▪ Chapter Overview

Like it or not, you can't escape politics. Every day around the world governments make decisions that affect our day-to-day lives. Politicians determine how much tax we pay, what laws we obey and how much money the state spends on essential services like roads, education and healthcare. The blog posts in this opening chapter examine public policy in a range of areas including trade, globalisation, regulation and taxation. There's also an insight into the politics of cyberspace and an explanation of voting systems.

international trade

International trade is the backbone of our modern commercial world. Every day, the buying and selling of goods and services occurs across national borders. No country can exist in isolation in a globalised world where goods, money and ideas move around the world faster and cheaper than ever before. The rise in international trade has fuelled the growth of globalisation.

The evidence of globalisation can be seen everywhere. In Australia, thanks to imports, we have access to a wide range of affordable yet quality products. We can go into a local store and buy a suit from Italy, a TV from Korea, an iPhone from China and flat pack furniture from Sweden. We benefit from the lower price of these items as they are made more cost-effectively overseas.

Due to our exports, people in other countries are eating our beef, drinking our wine, using our software, enjoying our tourism and riding in our fast ferries. Australia also exports its raw materials to the world. We have an abundance of natural resources that we cannot use and are able to sell the surplus to other countries, giving us a world market of seven billion people.

The difference in value between what a country imports and exports in goods and services is referred to as its *balance of trade*. A country has a trade deficit if it imports more than it exports and this is generally considered to be an unfavourable trade balance. A country has a trade surplus if it exports more than it imports which is generally considered to be a favourable trade balance.

As is typically the case in economics, there are differing views among economists about the pros and cons of trade imbalances. Asking whether trade deficits or surpluses are good or bad for an economy is like asking whether budget deficits or surpluses are good or bad for an economy - opinions are divided.

As I outlined in a recent post, *Government debt*, citizens around the world have been (erroneously) taught to believe that public debt is always bad. Conventional wisdom holds that borrowing money is foolhardy and that a prudent country, like a prudent person, should always rely on its own resources.

When it comes to trade, what is often misunderstood is that flows of trade involve flows of financial payments. Flows of international trade, therefore, are actually the same as flows of international capital. So the question becomes: Should we participate in global capital markets? The answer is unequivocally in the affirmative.

It makes economic sense for a national economy to borrow abroad, as long as the money is wisely invested in ways that raise a nation's economic growth over time. In Australia's case, our low levels of national savings forces businesses and governments to seek funds from overseas. Our long-standing dependence on foreign investment makes Australia a capital importer.

This vital and necessary capital has helped Australia become the world's 12th largest economy, boasting 23 years of uninterrupted growth. International capital has also enabled Australians to enjoy higher rates of economic growth, employment and standards of living than could have been achieved with domestic capital alone.

The equity in Australian companies is increasingly foreign owned. Not only that, but foreigners increasingly own our government debt. So yes, we are in hock to foreigners but we have been for most of our history. This should not be a cause for concern as foreign investment enables us to build infrastructure, develop industries and provide jobs.

A good example of this is our recent resources boom. The funding for this was sourced extensively from overseas. Foreigners saw it as a good investment opportunity. As a small country, Australia has and will continue to rely on foreign investment to build large-scale, capital-intensive industries. The capital we import, therefore, is being put to good use in fuelling productive activity.

Many economists (but certainly not all) believe that a trade deficit is not a problem in and of itself. However, as with most economic issues, there are no completely right or wrong answers. I'm in the camp that believes Australians benefit from the efficiencies, opportunities and consumer choices created in an economy which is open to world trade.

Australia was built on foreign investment, first from Britain, then America and more recently Japan and China. It is vital that Australia remains an attractive destination for foreign capital. Our way of life depends upon it.

Posting Date: 30 March 2015

foreign investment

International trade is the exchange of goods, services and capital among countries. The huge growth in world trade over recent decades has increased the economic interdependence between countries. Nations with strong international trade, like Australia, have become prosperous.

Australia is globally connected and international trade is an important part of our country's economy and its wealth. I explained in my post last week - *International trade* - that Australia runs a trade deficit, but I did not elucidate the link between our trade deficit and our current account deficit.

The terms "trade deficit" and "current account deficit" (CAD) are often used interchangeably. But they are not the same thing, albeit they are related. The CAD is a broader trade measure that encompasses the trade deficit along with other components. Let's examine each in turn.

A nation's *balance of trade* is the difference between its exports and imports. A country has a trade surplus if it exports more than it imports. A country has a trade deficit if it imports more than it exports. The trade balance is the largest component of the current account deficit or surplus.

The current account is the sum of the balance of trade (whether it's a surplus or deficit) + net factor income (such as interest and dividends) + net transfer payments (such as foreign aid and remittances abroad). Put simply, the current account records all transactions between Australia and the rest of the world.

In non-technical terms, when a country's current account balance is positive (running a surplus), the country is a net lender to the rest of the world. When a country's current account balance is negative (running a deficit), the country is a net borrower from the rest of the world.

Australia has a long history of sizeable current account deficits as our investment needs typically exceeded our domestic saving. We have made up this shortfall by borrowing abroad. This foreign capital - on which we have been absolutely dependent - has been used to finance our nation's development.

Foreign investment has brought many benefits including new jobs, greater innovation and access to markets abroad. We absolutely need other people's money as we have more economic opportunities than capital to service them. Yet many Australians are opposed to foreign ownership.

Unease among voters is fuelled by poorly informed commentary. Over recent times, the media has whipped the populace into a frenzy over Chinese investment in Australian agriculture. In the 1980s, the foreign ownership hysteria was targeted at Japanese investors, but that has since dissipated.

I acknowledge that foreigners becoming landowners over large tracts of rural Australia does not sit well with many Aussies. But farm sector investment is badly needed and it opens new export markets for the industry. So, why prevent productive investment which creates jobs and export earnings?

As noted in an illuminating article by Murdoch University academic, Anne Garnett, we clamour to keep foreign-owned car makers here, paying them billions of dollars to stay, while being wary of foreign investment in farms. This concern, she says, is unfounded as around 0.1% of foreign investment (in 2012) was in agriculture. She goes on to say that:

> Australia normally exports around two-thirds of total agricultural output each year. Even in a drought year we still export over half of what we produce. So Australia is in no danger of not being able to feed its people. Remember also that close to 90% of farmland

remains Australian-owned, so there is no possibility of all food being sold overseas.

Like any industry, agriculture requires capital, and it's going to require a lot more in the coming decades - and much of it will be imported. The same happened with the mining boom which was largely funded from money sourced from overseas. Foreigners saw it as a good investment opportunity.

Whether it's in farming, mining, manufacturing or other productive sectors, foreign investment is good for Australia and Australians. As we remain heavily reliant on capital inflows, we must ensure that Australia remains an attractive and welcoming investment environment.

Posting Date: 7 April 2015

governmentdebt

It's hard to think of a more emotive topic than government debt. Around the world citizens have been taught to believe that public debt is bad. Really? Deficits do matter but so does investing for the future as this generates benefits to society.

The notion that a budget surplus is always preferable to a budget deficit is too cut-and-dry. In reality, there are bad surpluses and good deficits. A bad surplus runs down services to the public by reining in public finances too hard. A good deficit borrows to fund investments in productive infrastructure.

[NB: There are two measures of sovereign debt: *current budget deficit* and *national public debt*. When a government spends more than it collects in any one year, a budget deficit exists. The accumulation of deficits over many years creates the national public debt.]

To use a medical analogy, debt is like cholesterol. Just as there is good cholesterol and bad cholesterol, there is good debt and bad debt. We need good cholesterol to keep our arteries clear and we need good debt to keep our finances healthy.

Over recent years my adult children have acquired debt - in fact, more debt than I personally have ever owed - and I could not be more proud of them. They have each used debt to buy a home. Household formation is a key driver of economic activity and my kids are playing their part.

Just as households go into debt to buy the things they can't swallow in one gulp, so do governments. Building essential public infrastructure like roads, airports, sewerage plants, hospitals and schools is very costly. Taxation revenue is often insufficient to fund infrastructure projects.

Of course, governments can increase personal and business taxes to cover any shortfall. But raising taxes is politically unpopular, plus it leaves taxpayers with less disposable income. It follows that if we have less to spend on goods and services, businesses and the broader economy will suffer.

A preferred way for governments to raise money is to issue bonds - i.e., borrow money today and pay it back in the future with interest. Some believe this is wrong as it leaves a debt for our children as future taxpayers. But if this debt is used to create a better world for our kids, is it such a bad thing?

The answer depends on whether the bonds will be used to fund productive investment or non-productive expenditure. Issuing bonds to improve a nation's transportation infrastructure which generates economic growth and leads to job creation is an example of "good" (productive) government debt.

Conversely, raising debt to pay for public welfare schemes is "bad" (unproductive) debt as it imposes a burden on the economy. Paying pensions and health care to an aging population does not facilitate economic growth or higher tax revenues but does provide a critical and necessary social safety net.

While debt is a four letter word, it's not necessarily a profanity. Yet in Australia, the deficit is at the top of the political agenda. Deficits are caused by government expenditure exceeding government revenue. Does that mean we have to slash government spending to fix the deficit?

The short answer is "no". In Australia, the greater issue to be addressed is not excessive expenditure but insufficient revenue. Put simply, we need to increase revenue by increasing taxation. Our current tax structure is fiscally unsustainable to cover necessary public spending.

As I stated in an earlier post, *A fairer tax system*, the low-hanging fruit in putting more funds in government coffers is the goods and services tax (GST). The GST is no longer a growth tax as household consumption has softened resulting in GST revenue not growing as fast as it once did.

While no one wants to pay more tax, it is inevitable that tax rates in Australia will rise. But that does not mean the end of deficits and debt. Governments have been borrowing for centuries and this will not change. Just as individuals need some level of debt throughout their lives, so do governments.

Posting Date: 9 February 2015

votingsystems

We all have our funny ways and one of my idiosyncrasies is a love of voting. It is a democratic right that I value and take seriously. I happily go to the polling booth to cast my vote for the party I wish to govern our nation. I believe that voting is a powerful way for citizens to have a say in the political decision making which affects their lives.

Australia is one of only a few countries in the world that has compulsory voting. While it is a civic duty for Aussies, I would still vote even if I was not compelled to do so. Proponents of compulsory voting argue that it produces a high voter turnout rate which more accurately reflects the will of the electorate and gives greater legitimacy to the government.

In contrast, opponents of compulsory voting assert that it is inconsistent with the freedoms associated with democracy. It is seen as an infringement of liberty and forces the ill-informed and those with little interest in politics to the polls. Critics believe that dragging politically apathetic citizens to the ballot booth to begrudgingly cast a vote is counter-productive.

I have sympathy with the notion that citizens should not be legally forced into the electoral process. Moreover, I understand the disenchantment people feel towards politicians. Further, I acknowledge the increasing disconnect between young people and democratic politics and their resentment of mainstream parties.

Ironically, while we in Australia debate whether voting should be voluntary, other nations debate whether it should be mandatory. The US has one of the lowest voter turnout rates of any developed nation which means that the voices of the disenfranchised are not heard. The UK is also struggling with falling voter turnout with younger people cynical about the significance of their vote.

Putting the mandatory/voluntary voting dichotomy aside, another issue which is periodically debated in Australia is the actual voting system we use. In the language of academics, many nations use a Plurality Voting System whereas, in Australia, we use a Ranked Voting System. Each system determines the way that votes are translated into seats in parliament.

The Plurality Voting System is a first-past-the-post system. Under this winner-takes-all system, electors vote for only one candidate and the candidate who receives the largest number of votes wins. A candidate is elected with a simple majority of votes (i.e., the highest number of votes in the count) but not necessarily more than half the votes.

While the Plurality System requires voters to choose only their first preference, a Ranked (aka Preferential) System requires voters to rank all candidates in order of their choice. Voters put the number 1 next to their first choice, 2 next to their second choice and so on. Candidates are elected outright if they gain more than half of the first preference (primary) votes.

If not, the candidate with the least first preferences is eliminated and their votes are redistributed according to the second or next available preference marked on the ballot paper. This process continues until one candidate has half of the votes and is elected. In this way, candidates build an absolute majority of support i.e., more than 50% of the votes.

An objection to the validity of preferential voting is that a candidate can win a seat with only a small percentage of the primary vote. This is because lower preferences can result in a "lowest common denominator" winner without much positive support of their own.

Preferential voting is a system largely unique to Australia. While I don't mind being told that I must vote (as I voluntarily would anyway), I don't like being forced to express a preference for all candidates. Invariably, I don't know every candidate on the ballot paper - particularly those who represent a single issue and/or a fringe micro party.

A better system, in my view, would be Optional Preferential Voting. Under such a system, I would have to express preferences only for the candidates I know and wish to vote for. No electoral system is perfect and people will find fault with any method used. However, I believe that Optional Preferential Voting would be a step in the right direction.

Posting Date: 6 October 2015

conductrisk

Some things are great in theory but difficult to implement in practice. Take, for example, the law in Australia and other parts of the world which requires directors and executives of financial institutions to be "fit and proper" persons. No argument with that - extreme care should be taken to ensure that those who manage other people's money are up to the task.

But how, in a practical sense, do you assess an individual's fitness and propriety to hold an executive position in banking? One criterion is education and training. A university degree in some business discipline is always well regarded. On top of this, you need some practical experience in the University of Hard Knocks. And it's really handy if you have a clean credit history and have never spent time in jail for fraud.

Well guess what? I suspect that every financial executive who wrote a subprime loan could tick all the boxes on the fit and proper test. And therein lies the problem - it doesn't measure greed and ambition. The executives on Wall Street and the organisations for which they worked did not have the right moral tone. This is why the root cause of the Global Financial Crisis (GFC) was not a failure of markets but a failure in corporate governance.

Greed is innate in human nature and Western society, in particular, places a high value on the pursuit of wealth and material possessions. Should we be surprised, then, that a culture of greed pervaded financial markets? The lust for success which drove the growth for growth sake mentality of the chiefs in the big corner offices created a moral crisis which, in turn, led to a financial one.

I find it ironic that the best and brightest caused the subprime crisis as they were too clever by half. Their hubris has made them sorry symbols of greed. Banking is an industry built on trust and the challenge facing regulators and boards is to devise a way of identifying and weeding out megalomaniacs with delusions of global domination. But this is easier said than done.

As I have opined before, the GFC was brought about by having the wrong people wedded to the wrong philosophy. It was not caused by a shortage of regulation. No sector of the business world is more heavily regulated than financial services. Yet, following the GFC, financial institutions around the world have been subjected to even greater regulation.

The harsh reality is that no set of rules can ensure the solvency of the banking system or its resilience in a crisis. Like driving a car, banking involves risks which can't be totally eliminated. Banking regulation will continue to evolve, punctuated by bursts of activity every time there is a serious crisis to manage. But regulation alone cannot change the hardwired primal human desire to conquer and succeed.

This is why conduct risk has become a hot topic in financial services. Conduct risk is defined as "the risk of inappropriate, unethical or unlawful behaviour on the part of an organisation's management or employees". It encompasses the risks associated with how an organisation and its employees conduct themselves and requires a focus on an organisation's corporate culture.

As children, we learned in Charles Dickens', *A Christmas Carol,* that greed is a bad thing. As adults, we were told by the character, Gordon Gekko, in the 1987 film, *Wall Street*, that "greed is good". The GFC brutally reminded us that unrestrained greed is not good and that extreme ambition, which some liken to a narcotic, can produce calamitous results.

At the end of the day, financial institutions need to find ways to measure greed, ambition and ethics as traditional numeric targets encourage and amplify unhealthy behaviours. I repeat, this is easier said than done!

Posting Date: 28 September 2015

defending globalisation

Free trade isn't widely accepted as completely beneficial to all parties. But history shows we all suffer when we revert to protectionism. One of the greatest lessons from the Great Depression is the catastrophic dangers of erecting trade tariffs.

Back then, countries retaliated against each other with trade barriers and this sent the world economy into a nosedive and helped cause a world war. Fast forward to today and the words of philosopher, George Santayana, are potent: "Those who cannot remember the past are condemned to repeat it."

To the shock and dismay of economists, nation states are again threatening to introduce import quotas in the hope of protecting domestic industry from foreign competition. Yet protectionism will harm the citizens of the world by causing a trade war which will bring global commerce to a halt.

This assault on free trade represents a grave political risk - it will actually cost jobs at a time when politicians face intense pressure to save domestic jobs. In January, world leaders flocked to Davo, Switzerland for the World Economic Forum and pledged to reject protectionism.

This promise flies in the face of a series of increased duties, re-imposed subsidies and a "Buy America" campaign by President Obama. Australian unions are also pushing for a "buy local" campaign. No wonder world trade ministers are worried.

The director-general of the World Trade Organisation has warned now is not the time for trade protectionism. British PM, Gordon Brown, has raised a similar concern about financial protectionism. Appealing to nationalist interests is destructive and all eyes will soon turn to the G20 Summit in

London as governments again discuss how to ease the pain of the crisis.

Perhaps the summit on April 2 should be billed as Bretton Woods Mark II as the rules which currently regulate the global economy need updating.

Eight decades ago, trade barriers helped turned a cyclical downturn into a Great Depression. History does not have to repeat itself. We are all part of one global village, so let's start behaving that way!

Posting Date: 16 March 2009

globalised politics

In 1938, Orson Welles narrated a now famous radio broadcast called *"War of the Worlds"*. This simulated radio news bulletin described what was happening in real time as Martians arrived on Earth. Of course, the broadcast was fictitious, but if extra-terrestrials did land on our planet, what would they make of us?

I'm confident that any galactic visitors would say we inhabit a stunningly beautiful planet. But when they learn how we have treated our home, I think they would struggle to believe that we are Earth's most intelligent life form. Moreover, when they discover our history of warfare, they would view human behaviour as light years away from how a civilised society should act.

As any student of history knows, it is not possible to study human history without studying armed conflict - the two are so interwoven. The rise and fall of empires and the division of national boundaries have largely been determined by the application of military force. The end result is that we have artificially divided our planet into 195 sovereign nations.

This divided citizenry is the root cause of many of our world's problems. We share one planet but are ordered along national lines. We act selfishly as citizens of independent nation-states instead of behaving selflessly as one united global family. By viewing the world through national-interest glasses, we fail to clearly see and deal with global issues.

The Great Depression is an example of this parochial thinking. After the 1929 stock market crash, nation-states sheltered their domestic industries from international competition and this led to a collapse in global demand. The Global Financial Crisis (GFC) again showed that we live in a borderless world. No country was immune from its effects even though some threatened to escape behind protectionist trade barriers - history repeating itself!

Just as the great oceans we navigate and the air we breathe know no national boundaries, so it is in a global economy. The challenge humanity faces is to better manage an interdependent world. International trade and commerce are moving us beyond a world order built around the sovereign state system. Additionally, the Internet is creating a global civilisation.

Futurists have long talked about the concept of a "Global Village" with "neighbours" electronically connected to each other. In this brave new integrated world, we are interconnected by an electronic nervous system. Today, economic transactions are not impeded by distance. With the click of a mouse, national borders can be transcended.

So, what are the politics of cyberspace? As social structures become transnational, will nation-states allow their borders to be deconstructed? Will multi-national corporations with their global brands eventually rule the world? Will the speed and power of technology and the rise of "de-localisation" render governments useless?

Just as I do not believe that robots are going to take over the world, I equally do not believe that national governments will disappear. In fact, I believe that nation-states will remain powerful actors in world affairs. They will still issue their own currency (Bitcoin will not take over the world!) and set the global agenda.

However, how territorial governments act in a borderless world will change. Co-ordinated action will increasingly be needed to tackle common problems and this is exactly what the G20 does. It deals with transnational issues that are beyond the remit of any single government to resolve. One of those issues is regulation of the global banking system.

The global regulatory standards on banking supervision are set out in what are known as the Basel Accords. These accords have the laudable objective of increasing the stability of global financial markets. My views of the Basel regulations are outlined in two previous posts - *Global banking laws* and *Regulation gone mad*.

Whether it's roundtables on banking regulation or summits on climate change, we can expect to see a rise in the activity of international co-ordinating bodies. The G20 - as the world's premier forum for economic co-operation - has a critical role to play in ensuring that bodies like the World Bank, the OECD and the IMF operate effectively and facilitate coherent global economic policy-making.

True global co-operation and consensus is possible and my hope is that this co-operative form of international governance becomes the new world order.

Posting Date: 27 April 2015

government bureaucracy

The Australian federal government knows how much I earn because my financial details are lodged with the Australian Taxation Office. The NSW state government knows when I came into this world as my birth is registered with the Registry of Births, Deaths and Marriages. My local shire council knows where I live because my address details are recorded in the register of rate payers.

Governments know everything about us, yet there is a lack of integration and co-ordination between the various branches and levels of government. Public administration is fragmented and is characterised by demarcation disputes, competing imperatives and a silo mentality. Typically, the left hand does not know what the right is doing. A simple example will help here.

Following the last local council elections, my daughter received a *Penalty Notice For Failure To Vote* from the NSW Division of the Australian Electoral Commission (AEC). Leanne had written 12 months earlier to the AEC informing them she was temporarily moving to London. As it transpired, the AEC had not informed its NSW branch that Leanne would be out of the country.

So, I contacted Leanne in London and asked her to send me the e-mail she had received a year earlier from the AEC. I then phoned the NSW branch and naïvely thought they would (i) apologise for their error and (ii) accept the email note from their national office. Wrong! I had to complete and lodge a declaration telling the NSW branch what their national office already knew!

Now imagine if a private sector organisation made a mistake and then forced the customer to do the running around in correcting their error. You would likely take your business elsewhere as choice is one of the great features of a free market economy. Regrettably, choice does not exist where governments are the monopoly provider and competition is not allowed.

I acknowledge that the size and complexity of our three-level system of government makes seamless public sector service delivery a real challenge. But we just can't throw our hands in the air and say it's all too hard. Building a strong economy and a vibrant society requires the involvement of all government agencies working co-operatively together.

The federal government, quite rightly, is encouraging the private sector to improve productivity. As I explained in my post, *The productivity paradox*, this means producing more with less by becoming more efficient. But shouldn't the government also try to work smarter and eliminate waste? Unfortunately, when it comes to our political leaders, it's a case of do as I say, not as I do.

Why shouldn't ministers be judged on their own productivity performance and that of the ministries they represent? The classic response is that public sector outputs are difficult to measure. Many public servants work on back-office activities that don't directly affect the public. The end result is a public sector that is inherently inefficient by private sector economic standards.

It seems to me that one way to make great strides in achieving greater public sector productivity is to eliminate a layer of government. As I opined in an earlier post, *Have state governments passed their use by date?*, no system of democracy is perfect - but surely we can do better than what we currently have in place.

What governments can immediately do to improve private sector productivity is reduce government red tape and regulation. The regulatory and compliance burden on all Australian industries is onerous. We need rules that allow business to be flexible and innovative. Perhaps we could start with a more flexible industrial relations system and a more competitive tax system.

In an enlightening opinion piece - *Australia's productivity problem: why it matters* - Professor John Freebairn from the University of Melbourne underscores that "increasing productivity involves all of us: politicians, bureaucrats, business managers, employees and households". I'm not convinced that politicians and bureaucrats truly understand their role in improving productivity.

Posting Date: 25 February 2013

financial sector

The financial services industry touches the lives and wallets of virtually every Australian. Whether it's taking out a mortgage to buy a home, obtaining capital to start a business, transferring money to electronically pay bills, putting savings away to fund your retirement or insuring your life and personal possessions, the financial services industry is there to help.

Our finance industry encompasses a broad range of organisations that deal with the flow and management of money. These organisations include banks, building societies, credit unions, credit card issuers, insurance companies, superannuation providers, investment managers, stock broking firms, financial consultants and advisers.

The Australian financial services sector performs a pivotal role in providing credit to all other sectors in the Australian economy. Businesses, households and governments often take on debt in order to grow. (I explained the role of credit-driven growth in an earlier post, *In defence of deficits*.) Thus, the financial services sector provides the financing that fuels economic growth.

The health of our finance industry and the economy are inseparable. Financial development leads to economic growth as it enables businesses to start up, expand and compete in local and international markets. In short, the financial services industry is the hub of the Australian economy, facilitating the productive flow of funds between sectors, companies and individuals.

According to the Financial Services Council, financial services account for almost 11% of Australia's GDP. This compares to 10.3% for mining and 7.6% for manufacturing. It is the largest sector of the Australian economy, directly employing 420,000 people. The finance industry pays the highest average rate of corporate tax of any industry in Australia.

Underpinning much of Australia's financial services strength is the growth of its investment funds sector. As I stated last week, Australia's superannuation funds represent the fourth largest pool of investment funds in the world. Some of these funds are now being used to fund infrastructure. Infrastructure is critical to Australia's national productivity and economic growth.

No matter which way you look at it, the financial services industry plays a key role in facilitating economic growth in Australia. Indeed, it would be difficult for any economic activity to take place without financial services. The industry survived the shockwaves of the Global Financial Crisis (GFC) relatively unscathed and can make an even bigger contribution to Australian society.

However, as is the case across all industry sectors, the cost and complexity of regulation is crippling productivity growth at a national and industry level. The GFC fuelled calls for greater regulation of banking and finance. Yet no sector of the business world is more heavily regulated or supervised than financial services.

As I opined recently in *Regulation gone mad*, efforts by regulators to bolster financial system stability and avoid a repeat of the GFC turmoil are laudable. Few would challenge the goal of a more resilient banking sector. But care must be taken not to punish those, like mutuals, which did not engage in the reckless behaviour that contributed to the GFC.

Also, at a time when manufacturing is in decline and the resources boom is fading, financial services can play a significant role in Australia's export growth. In this area the government needs to act to bring about tax reform. Overseas investors are reluctant to place money with domestic fund managers due to prevailing uncertainties in the Australian tax law.

Australia's financial services industry is strong and sophisticated. The work it does is vital and fundamental. It operates with the trust and confidence of its stakeholders. The outputs it produces contribute to the quality of life for working and retired Australians. The Australian financial industry is truly the engine room of our nation's growth and development.

Posting Date: 10 June 2013

population policies

In 1935 Prime Minister, Billy Hughes, admonished Australians to "populate or perish". Seventy-five years later our population has risen to 22 million and is predicted to reach 35 million by 2050. Meanwhile, global population is set to hit 7 billion early in 2012 and 9.1 billion in 2050.

Every year mother Earth welcomes over 100 million more babies and there is fierce debate about the pros and cons of this level of growth. As a general rule, environmental groups want little growth while economists argue for rapid growth. The population debate intersects with many others and is not a simple, one-dimensional issue.

In Australia, the former coalition government introduced a baby bonus to encourage parents to have THREE kids. As Peter Costello put it: "One for mum, one for dad and one for the country." Australia is currently in the midst of a mini baby boom. The ABS estimates Australia's population is bolstered by one birth every one minute and 44 seconds.

In contrast, the British based think-tank, Optimum Population Trust (OPT), is encouraging Britains to stop at TWO children. The OPT has warned of the dire consequences of human proliferation. On his appointment as a patron of the OPT, Sir David Attenborough said the growth in global population was "frightening".

Meanwhile in China, the government introduced its ONE child policy in 1979. It is estimated that had China not introduced her policy limiting couples to one child, there would be 400 million more Chinese than there are today. The unintended consequence of this policy, however, is that China's population is getting too old, too fast.

The real population explosion is occurring in third world countries. Population grows fastest in poorest countries as high fertility rates are strongly correlated with poverty. However, according to a recent report, third world population growth does not contribute significantly to rising greenhouse gas emissions as poor countries have low emissions.

Paul Ehrlich's predictions of mass starvation did not come true in his 1968 book, *The Population Bomb*. Nonetheless, modern day doomsayers are warning it's a case of populate and perish. Overpopulation is cited as the root cause of climate change and is said to be testing the limits of social, economic and environmental sustainability.

Clearly, population growth is a big topic and I can only provide a brief treatment of it here. The issues are complex and have multiple variables.

Posting Date: 25 January 2010

taxation reform

Australia is long overdue for a mature debate about the critical need to reform its taxation system. History shows that achieving meaningful reform will be a political, economic and social minefield. But it's a debate we must have if we are to avert a fiscal crisis and ensure our nation's long-term economic viability.

As citizens, we expect governments to provide essential services. However, as taxpayers, we are reluctant to put more revenue into government coffers from our personal incomes. We must break this impasse as our current taxation structures are not economically sustainable.

With a growing and aging population, taxes need to rise to cover increased public spending. We need more schools, more hospitals, more roads and the list goes on. Without an increase in government receipts we are setting ourselves up for permanent structural deficits.

Any review of taxation (including welfare payments) should seek to share the burden of reform fairly across the community. Of course, fairness and equity in taxation are like beauty - they're in the eye of the beholder. When it comes to taxation, the beholders are typically categorised as either rich or poor.

This rich/poor divide is unhelpful and - as noted in an October 2014 article by former government minister, Amanda Vanstone - stirs up the politics of envy. She writes:

> Daily we are invited to assume that wealthier people are creeps, tax cheats and the cause of others among us being poorer. It is undoubtedly true that some wealthier people are creeps, tax cheats, selfish and carry any number of other unattractive traits. Equally there will be poorer people who are bash-up artists,

druggies and thieves. In both cases, they are the exception rather than the norm.

Vanstone contends that the so-called rich get a pretty rough deal in terms of media coverage. She argues that the top end of town do most of the heavy lifting when it comes to their share of the tax burden. She points out that "... just 2% of taxpayers pay more than 25% of all income tax. The rest of us should be delighted these people have done so well economically".

Australian demographer, Bernard Salt, picked up this theme in an article he penned on 26 February, 2015 for *The Australian* newspaper titled *Inconvenient truth on tax a bit rich*. Citing Australian Taxation Office (ATO) data for the year ended June 2012, Salt notes that Australians on higher incomes do, quite rightly, pay more tax. He goes on to say that:

> The confronting, unpalatable and inconvenient truth that flows from the income and income-tax data published by the ATO is that the rich do indeed pay tax. In fact, the rich pay income tax that is 13 times more than their proportionate share by population, and which most Australians would probably say is fair enough.

The myth that the rich don't pay their share of taxes was also the subject of an article by the *Daily Telegraph's* Chief Political Reporter, Simon Benson. Drawing on Bernard Salt's article the day before, Benson lamented that "today in Australia there is nothing more political, nothing that more crudely seeks to divide classes, than taxation".

Benson says that under our taxation system, anyone on $180,000 p.a. is considered rich as they fall into the same tax bracket as billionaires. While he acknowledges that $180k is a lot of money, he underscores that it is barely rich.

"The argument the barely rich should pay more tax because they earn too much money or are engaged in some sort of elaborate tax avoidance scheme is the great political folly," says Benson.

The Federal Government has prepared a White Paper on Tax Reform and has promised to take to the next election any recommendations it adopts from the Paper. Business groups, trade unions, welfare agencies and taxation experts will all have a view as to how to make the taxation system fairer and simpler. Broad community discussion is appropriate and should be welcomed.

My hope is that the conversations about tax reform are informed and intelligent. However, my suspicion is that it will be a very taxing and emotive debate.

Posting Date: 16 March 2015

political discontent

History shows that economic hardship and rising unemployment drive civil unrest. Whenever the populace feels sufficiently downtrodden, violent protests erupt, which is why the Global Financial Crisis (GFC) has sparked a wave of demonstrations around the world.

People are angry and scared and venting their anxiety over an uncertain future. Riots have rocked China and the IMF chief has issued a warning about on-going protests. Global capitalism is increasingly seen as the enemy of the people and this is fuelling social discontent.

Policymakers need to be careful that this unrest does not lead to war. World stability hangs by a thread and tensions are running high. Politicians are trying to avert a disaster but the class warfare between the rich and the poor shows no signs of abating.

Many ideological battle lines have been drawn in this social politics of rage. Bailing out Wall Street is seen as a cop out by Main Street. The new deal is viewed as a raw deal. The left is challenging the right. Poor workers are bitter at their rich bosses. Democrats are facing off against republicans while labour versus the liberals.

Waleed Aly, a lecturer in politics at Monash University, has written an instructive piece on the social and political consequences of the GFC. In his article, *"Beneath the financial crisis waits a nastier beast"*, he makes a number of compelling observations about how people behave in times of great insecurity.

With worldwide job losses predicted to be in the tens of millions, living standards for many on this planet will plummet. Poverty will rise, social disturbances will continue and leading economist, Nouriel Roubini, is even warning of food riots in America. (Note: Roubini is one of the few economists who actually predicted the credit crisis.)

This Saturday our nation will pause to commemorate the Anzac spirit. Lest we forget that the Great Depression fuelled the rise of radical political movements in the run up to World War II. Let's hope that history does not repeat itself and that extremist groups are not successful in pursuing their political agendas on the back of the current social discontent.

Posting Date: 20 April 2009

ancient wisdom

Many consider that Socrates' most important contribution to Western thought is his dialectic method of inquiry, known as the Socratic method. This Classical Greek philosopher found that his students learned more when he asked them a series of questions in lieu of just giving them the answer.

By challenging his students' beliefs through questioning, Socrates enabled them to think through issues by themselves. The influence of this approach is evident today throughout society. Significantly, it is used to develop scientific theories in which hypothesis is the first stage.

To solve a problem using the Socratic method, one need only pose a series of questions and the answer, so they say, will filter out. Socrates applied his problem solving method to the examination of key moral concepts such as good and justice.

The Global Financial Crisis (GFC) and the subsequent economic downturn raised a range of important and fundamental questions. In the Socratic tradition of nurturing debate, a number of my blog posts over the past year deliberately challenged readers to think critically about the social and economic implications of the GFC.

I hope my Socratic questions about globalism, capitalism, socialism, ethics, greed and human behaviour have helped us emerge from the financial crisis with a better understanding and defence of our beliefs. In the process, I trust I have added to the richness of the economic debate.

George Bernard Shaw wrote: "You see things and you say, 'Why?' But I dream things that never were and I say, 'Why not?'" My (utopian) dream is for a wisdom-based global economy characterised by humanity thinking and acting as one global community. To achieve this dream, world leaders must facilitate and actively support more Socratic dialogue on global threats and opportunities.

The future of sovereign nations has already become the focus of debate. This is because the growing interdependence of a global economy is increasingly undermining the independence of nation-states in setting social and economic policies.

The time to act is now. The age of ignorance must come to an end. The key Socratic question is: Can humanity change its ways? I believe we can. As we enter the period of peace and goodwill to all, my Christmas wish in this, my penultimate blog post for 2009, is for this rhetoric to be turned into an agenda for action.

Posting Date: 14 December 2009

02 Economic Trends

▪▪ Chapter Overview

Economics is a social science. It is the study of human nature as it applies to money. Economists analyse the behaviour of individual people and firms within an economy (microeconomics) and examine the economic activity of an entire country (macroeconomics). When it comes to money we do not always make rational choices and, as explained in a number of the blog posts in this chapter, this contributed to the Global Financial Crisis. Other topics covered include consumer confidence, personal debt, spending patterns, money management, property prices, interest rates and household savings.

icelandic economics

It was the most destructive financial shock since the Great Depression and it brought the free market to the precipice. The Global Financial Crisis (GFC) started as a localised issue in the US housing market and quickly escalated into a catastrophic global meltdown.

From continent to continent, stocks plunged, margin calls rose, banks collapsed, consumer confidence dived and reputations suffered. Fear and panic reached epidemic levels as trust in the global financial system plummeted.

Banks limited the supply of credit, consumers tightened their purse strings and governments spent unprecedented amounts on various forms of assistance. To avoid a systemic collapse, bank bailouts were the order of the day in some countries, but not in Iceland.

No other country exploded more quickly and spectacularly than Iceland during the onset of the GFC. The Icelandic economy suffered one of the deepest meltdowns in the world. What Iceland did in response flew in the face of conventional economic wisdom.

The frozen island took the polar opposite approach to the US and Europe and let its three major banks collapse. Iceland refused to bail out the Icelandic banks in order to shield taxpayers from footing the bill for irresponsible lending practices. It also introduced measures to help indebted homeowners.

Famed for its active volcanoes and lava fields, Iceland is now famous (infamous?) for rising from the ashes following the collapse of its banking system in 2008. While the "let them fail policy" drove a turnaround in Iceland's economy, its unorthodox approach drew both praise and criticism.

Those who hold up Iceland as the poster child for how a

nation ought to respond to a major economic crisis argue that supporting households was more important than protecting bondholders. In short, forcing losses onto bank creditors was seen as the preferable thing to do.

Not surprisingly, international financial institutions took a diametrically opposite view. They remain critical of Iceland's decision not to honour its financial obligations. The damage inflicted on foreign creditors, investors and depositors in Icelandic banks tarnished Iceland's reputation.

By way of background, during the 1900s and early 2000s, Iceland tried to become a "Nordic Tiger". Its political leaders opened Iceland to the global economy. The dire state of the local fishing industry drove a series of sweeping economic reforms accompanied by a foray into global banking.

Iceland privatised its banks, signed the European Free Trade Agreement and moved from a fixed exchange rate system to a floating Krona. The country (including households and businesses) then went into overdrive in borrowing and spending.

Between 2000 and 2007, domestic credit in the Icelandic banking system more than quadrupled as a share of GDP. Icelanders were able to access easy credit which resulted in escalating house prices and soaring consumption.

When the banks collapsed in 2008, Icelanders paid dearly for their extravagant ways with the savings of 50,000 local people wiped out. Moreover, the stock market plunged 90%, unemployment rose ninefold and inflation skyrocketed past 18%.

Citizens of other nations also suffered. Once privatised, the three Icelandic banks looked overseas for growth as the domestic economy of 300,000 people was considered too small. Iceland opened high-interest online bank accounts, attracting almost 500,000 customers throughout Europe.

Many of these were British and Dutch depositors and the collapse of the Icelandic banks left the UK and the Netherlands with significant costs. The (then) UK Prime Minister, Gordon Brown, announced that his government would launch legal action against Iceland on behalf of the 300,000 UK savers.

Interestingly, the Icelandic banks did not go broke by buying worthless subprime securities. They obtained their money largely from international investors and the interbank lending markets, making them heavily dependent on foreign capital. These funding sources dried up in 2008 at which stage the foreign debt of the Icelandic banks had grown to over eight times GDP.

The unique path that Iceland took in 2008 raises ethical questions about responsibility. I believe that individuals, corporations and governments have a moral obligation to do all they can to honour their financial commitments. Iceland broke this rule and got away with it, but does that make it right?

Yes, the Icelandic banks were reckless but so were Icelanders who became unsustainably wealthier prior to the crash by taking on record amounts of debt to income. Taxpayers are also voters and Icelanders knowingly voted in a reformist government that sided with bankers and allowed cavalier behaviour.

While many see Iceland's decision to default on their debt to foreign financiers as some sort of Viking victory for the people, I think it sets a dangerous precedent. Iceland did not come up with a new economic disaster management plan, but a regrettable way to wipe the slate clean.

Posting Date: 25 May 2015

introductoryeconomics

Right now you are reading this blog, but you could be doing something else like taking a nap. You can't do those two things at once, so you gave up the chance for a snooze to peruse this post. In other words, you made a choice among alternatives about how you would spend your time (a finite resource).

According to economists, every choice we make has an opportunity cost. The term opportunity cost is defined as "the cost of an alternative that must be forgone in order to pursue a certain action". Put simply, it's what a person sacrifices when they choose one option over another.

Let's say you have $100 in your purse. You can spend it on a pair of jeans or a meal. You choose to buy the denim jeans, so the opportunity cost is the restaurant meal you cannot afford. For everything you choose to do, there's something else you won't be able to do.

Every day as consumers, we are forced to make choices due to "scarcity". Scarcity and opportunity cost are two interlinking economic concepts. Economists view the world through the lens of scarcity. Indeed, without scarcity, the science of economics would not exist.

Scarcity arises because as a society we have unlimited wants but limited resources. We all know you can't have everything you want - we have to choose and make trade-offs. Economics is the study of how individuals, firms and nations deal with the limitations imposed by scarcity.

Scarcity does not just involve choices about consumable goods. Scarcity also applies to time, resources, information and even space. Let's say you are going on a holiday and have only a finite amount of room in your bag. You must choose what to pack and what not to pack as the space available is scarce.

It's not just individuals who can't have everything they want. Businesses with limited capital must choose between spending more on innovation or on marketing. Similarly, governments must make choices about spending priorities - more on health and less on education?

It can be seen that the science of economics does not just focus on money and business. Rather, it examines how individuals, businesses and governments make the best possible choices to get what they want, and how those choices interact with markets.

Contemporary economic theory is premised on the assumption that we make rational and prudent choices. Rational choice is defined as "people making calculated, self-interested choices after weighing the costs and benefits of those choices".

The harsh reality is that humans do not obey the efficient, orderly principals espoused by free-market thinkers. When it comes to money, we often act irrationally and make poor choices. The Global Financial Crisis (GFC) provided a dramatic demonstration of our flawed decision making.

Many people in the US bought houses at grossly inflated prices and expected their value to keep rising. In the process, borrowers saddled themselves with loans they could not afford, which led to the subprime mortgage meltdown and ultimately the catastrophic GFC.

This "irrational exuberance" (the now infamous phrase coined by Alan Greenspan) was not confined to the household sector. Borrowers, bankers and brokers were united in the delusional belief that house prices never go south.

It's clear that we humans are far too emotive for rational

economic models to accurately predict our behaviour which is why much of the foundation of modern economics needs to be re-thought. Post GFC, many people have turned to behavioural economics to understand what happened.

Behavioural economics combines psychology and economics to explain how people really make decisions when they spend, invest, save and borrow money. Behavioural economists have shown that real-world people are irrational and struggle to exert control over their emotions and impulses.

Traditional economists and behavioural economists do not always see eye-to-eye. Economists, of course, are famous for disagreeing among themselves (e.g., Keynesians versus Monetarists). Thus, the old joke about the economics profession being the only field where two people can win a Nobel Prize for saying the exact opposite thing!

Posting Date: 16 November 2015

olympic economics

In August, the Games of the XXXI Olympiad will be held in Rio de Janeiro. The 2016 Summer Olympics will reportedly cost Brazil over US$14 billion. The South American nation won a highly-contested race to host the world's most expensive quadrennial sporting event.

Hosting this mega-sport extravaganza is a financially risky proposition as each edition invariably costs more than planned. An Oxford University study examining the Olympic Games from 1962 to 2012 discovered that host cities, on average, experience a 179% cost overrun during the preparation phase.

The gold medal for Olympic financial disasters goes to Montreal in Canada. The cost blowout for the 1976 Games was a massive 796% which nearly bankrupted the city. Montreal's Olympic legacy was a $1 billion debt which took 30 years to pay off.

At an estimated cost of US$42 billion, the 2008 Beijing Games earned the title of the most expensive Summer Games ever. The Games drove massive investment in new infrastructure but came at a huge human cost. Money was diverted away from social programs addressing poverty and over two million residents were displaced to make way for urban redevelopment.

What Beijing spent on its Games was eclipsed six years later by Russia. The 2014 Sochi Winter Olympics cost an astronomical US$50 billion. The Games, which were plagued by widespread waste and corruption, did not deliver the promised economic benefits and failed to turn the Black Sea resort into a tourist mecca.

Hosting the Olympics is clearly a high-risk game. Many see it as an economic gamble which rarely delivers "gold" payback to taxpayers. Indeed, the privilege of putting on the world's biggest sporting party is generally a bittersweet experience. The short-term prestige of basking in the global spotlight is normally overshadowed by long-term economic burdens.

After the athletes have left and the Olympic bunting has been taken down, high-priced sports facilities often become ghost towns. Host cities typically struggle to find a productive use of the dozens of venues which have been built - as is the case with Beijing's Bird's Nest and Water Cube and many of the venues built for the Athens Games.

Moreover, there is little evidence to support the conventional wisdom that the host city benefits from a large boost in overseas tourism following the Games. Paradoxically, most host cities find that tourism actually falls during the Games. Olympic tourists replace normal tourists who stay away to avoid the congestion and greater expense during the Games.

The inconvenient truth is that the financial benefits of hosting the five-ring circus are exaggerated and short-lived. Economic impact studies invariably show that the Games are a money pit, not a cash cow. As Olympic Games rarely turn a profit, they are not seen by economic rationalists as a wise investment.

Something that is routinely overlooked by organisers when modelling the cost of running the Games is what economists call "opportunity cost". This is defined as "the cost of an alternative that must be forgone in order to pursue a certain action". So, instead of spending lavishly on hosting the Olympics, a nation could re-direct those funds - which don't come out of thin air - to much needed public works like schools and hospitals.

If what lies at the end of the Olympic bidding race is fool's gold, why do so many nations fall over themselves to be the host city? Is a moment in the global sporting sun worth the multi-billion dollar price tag? Clearly, many nations think so, but their real motives are not economic.

Broadly speaking, most nations host the Olympics for fame and prestige. More specifically, the Beijing games were intended to show off China's spending and organisational power. The Sochi Games were designed to be a symbol of Putin's international legitimacy. And the Rio Games are an opportunity for the emerging nation of Brazil to display its ability to play host to the rest of the world.

Some cities are starting to question the merits of hosting the Olympics. Last year, Boston withdrew its bid to host the 2024 Summer Olympics, citing concerns about cost. Similarly, the IOC chose from an abnormally small pool of candidates for the 2022 Winter Olympics after several European cities, including Oslo and Krakow, withdrew their candidacy.

Cities seem less enthusiastic today about hosting the Olympics. The 2004 Games attracted 12 applicant cities, whereas the 2020 Games had just five. Given this shrinking pool, there are now calls for the long-standing host city rotation system to be replaced by a permanent venue for future Games. That sounds like an Olympic winning idea to me.

Posting Date: 28 March 2016

moneycreation

The world as we know it would not function without money. Money is an essential human creation and everyone uses it. Money has a powerful influence on our lives and we have an emotional connection to it. Money keeps us awake at night and motivates us to work hard during the day.

We can't live without money, yet few people can precisely tell you what it is and how it works. Defining money is surprisingly difficult as it does not just comprise paper currency. In Australia, physical cash accounts for less than 4% of "broad money" (i.e., the amount of money held by households and companies in bank deposits and currency).

These days, very few of us are paid in cash. Our salaries and wages are credited to our bank or credit union account. Which is one of the reasons why 96% of broad money exists in bank deposits. This form of electronic money can't be physically held as it is intangible numbers in a ledger.

These numbers are accounting entries and banks produce a large percentage of them when they create new money by lending money. As counter-intuitive as it sounds, most money is lent into existence. Banks and other financial institutions create new money whenever they extend credit.

Banks are in the business of selling credit. Money is created as evidence of debt. Credit and debt are the same thing, seen from different points of view. Money is a debt instrument, not a debt itself. Thus, the amount of money in our economy is a function of debt.

This debt is created when a government borrows from its central bank. It is also created when individual citizens of a sovereign nation go into debt by taking out loans from banks and other financial institutions through the mechanism of Fractional Reserve Banking.

When a bank makes a loan to a customer, the proceeds are deposited to an account in the name of the borrower or in the name of the person/s from whom goods or services (e.g., car, holiday) are being purchased. Regardless, new credit money is created and this increases the money supply.

However, only a fraction of the new credit money which is deposited is kept in reserve to meet withdrawals. The rest is invested by banks in loans to other customers (borrowers). This is known as Fractional Reserve Banking and it is the current form of banking worldwide.

The amount of money a bank can lend is affected by the cash reserve or liquidity requirement set by the local banking authority. Liquidity refers to the amount of cash a bank holds to meet its financial obligations (like customer withdrawals) as they come due.

Let's say the cash reserve (liquidity) requirement is 10% of a bank's total deposits. This means the bank can lend $90 when it receives a $100 deposit. That $90 is used by the borrower to buy goods and the shopkeeper deposits the funds with his bank.

The second bank takes the $90, keeps 10% and lends $81 to another person. That $81 goes back into the economy and eventually finds its way into the other person's account at a third bank. The third bank, in turn, holds back $8.10 and lends out $72.90.

This goes on until there is nothing left to deposit and lend out. If you do the math, you will find that the original $100 eventually amounts to $1,000 in credit money. This is an example of the money multiplier effect resulting from banks creating money through their lending activities.

It can be seen that how money is actually created today (a) differs from the description found in some economics textbooks and (b) dispels the myth that financial institutions can only lend out pre-existing money. Banks create "cashless money" from making loans which means that money is really just an IOU.

When the average Joe learns that banks make money seemingly "out of thin air" they are either surprised or sceptical. For the Doubting Thomases out there, I'll leave the final comment on money creation to none other than the Bank of England. In a 2014 report the bank stated:

> In the modern economy, most money takes the form of bank deposits. But how those bank deposits are created is often misunderstood: the principal way is through commercial banks making loans. Whenever a bank makes a loan, it simultaneously creates a matching deposit in the borrower's bank account, thereby creating new money.

So, now you know how money is created in reality.

Posting Date: 2 February 2015

money manufacture

A government can make money by literally making money as the business of minting metal coins and printing paper banknotes is profitable. Since the cost of manufacturing currency is low, the face value of currency is much larger than its cost of production. The value of currency over its cost of production is called seigniorage.

The word seigniorage comes from Old French and means the right of a feudal lord or ruler - *seigneur* - to mint money. In the Middle Ages, kings, dukes and counts exercised the privilege to coin money. In modern societies, the monopoly rights of seigniorage - the revenue earned from issuing legal tender - belongs to governments.

Around the world, it costs less than a dollar to print/mint a dollar. For illustrative purposes, let's say a sovereign nation adds five cents of ink to ten cents of paper and labels the end product a $50 bill. The government has just made $49.85. If that same bill had a face value of $100, the government's profit from seigniorage would rise to $99.85.

We all intuitively know that the currency we have in our wallets and purses has no intrinsic value in and of itself. Banknotes are just colourful pieces of paper with ink patterns used to represent different denominations. But paper money has implicit monetary value as it can be exchanged by the bearer for goods and services.

It is this difference between the value in use (cost of production) and value in exchange (face value) that generates seigniorage. As the cost of producing larger denominations is about the same as smaller denominations, the seigniorage of larger bills is more than smaller bills.

Money that is not backed by a real commodity (such as gold) is called fiat money. Most modern paper currencies are fiat currencies which is why it's said that paper money has no intrinsic value. Currency is valuable because everyone believes it's valuable and therefore accepts it in payment for goods and services. In essence, the value of money is upheld by collective faith.

The Reserve Bank of Australia (RBA) issues currency notes and the Commonwealth Treasury issues coins (produced by the Royal Australian Mint). The seigniorage earned on coin issue is considerably less than that earned on notes. The value of coin outstanding in Australia is currently around $5 billion compared with around $65 billion in notes outstanding.

When an Australian bank requires additional banknotes, it buys them from the RBA. The bank pays for these notes by providing the RBA with another financial asset - such as a government security - the value of which is equal to the face value of the notes. Seigniorage arises because the cost of producing the notes is much smaller than the value of the asset received by the RBA.

In a fiat monetary system there is no restraint on the amount of money that can be created. This allows unlimited credit creation. Post-GFC, some nations used quantitative easing (QE) to create new money. QE is often described as "printing money" but this is incorrect. With QE, there is no need to crank up the printing presses and put crisp new bills into circulation.

Using QE, a country can create new sums of money (non-cash) out of thin air. Its central bank simply uses a computer to transfer funds to itself. The central bank utilises its new central bank reserves to buy assets - government and corporate bonds. The financial institutions selling the assets have the "new" money deposited into their accounts which boosts the money supply.

QE produces money electronically. The greatest amount of

seigniorage results from the electronic creation of money, since virtually any amount of money can be created electronically at modest cost. This is why the profits of the US Federal Reserve have risen markedly in recent years. The Fed has created more money than usual and has invested it in higher-paying assets.

It can be seen that governments and central banks - as issuers of paper money, manufacturers of metal coins and originators of electronic money - benefit financially from the money they create. However, there is a third actor in the money creation game - the banking sector. In most advanced economies, the majority of money is lent into existence.

As I explained in an earlier post, *Money creation*, banks and other financial institutions create new money whenever they extend credit. The creation of non-cash money by granting loans might be loosely described as "private seigniorage". Economists do not measure private seigniorage but, as with public seigniorage income, it's a "licence to print money".

Posting Date: 23 November 2015

cashless society

Cold hard physical currency is on the endangered species list. Whether cash ever becomes completely extinct is subject to debate. What is clear is that cash is no longer king due to the rise in electronic payments. Notes and coins are increasingly giving way to tap-and-pay.

The move to cashless payments was driven initially by magnetic-stripe cards, then by the Internet and now by mobile pay technology. The use of cash is diminishing rapidly and the amount of cash in circulation, relatively speaking, has fallen.

According to the World Payments Report 2015 by Capgemini, 357.9 billion non-cash transactions were made globally in 2013. In terms of value, 2013/14 was a watershed period with some countries reporting that cashless payments had overtaken cash transactions for the first time.

In Canada, the number of cash transactions fell to 43.9% in 2013. In the United Kingdom, 52% of payment transactions in 2014 were non-cash. In Australia, 53% of payments are now done with cards or mobile payment apps.

Denmark wants to totally eradicate cash payments. The Danish government recently announced proposals to allow shops, restaurants and petrol stations to refuse payments in cash. Customers are now required to use contactless debit cards or some other means of electronic payment.

The Danes hope to go completely cashless during 2016. This would make them the first nation in the world to entirely abandon paper currency in favour of electronic money. Denmark's Nordic neighbours, Sweden and Norway, are in hot pursuit to become cashless.

Scandinavians rely on cash for less than 6% of all payments

made. In contrast, around 47% of US payments are still made with cash. According to the Danish Bankers Association, a cashless society is "no longer an illusion but a vision that can be fulfilled within a reasonable time frame".

As an interesting aside, Sweden's highest profile cash-free advocate is former ABBA member, Björn Ulvaeus. After his son was robbed several years ago, Ulvaeus became an evangelist for the electronic payment movement, claiming that cash was the primary cause of crime.

Someone else who believes that paper money facilitates crime is Harvard economist, Ken Rogoff. In a 2014 article, Rogoff argued that eliminating cash would allow law enforcement agencies to crack down on illicit activities, as the anonymous nature of paper money fuels the underground economy.

Rogoff also posited that taking cash out of circulation would eliminate the problem referred to by economists as the zero lower bound. This impacts the operation of monetary policy and arises when a central bank tries to reduce the interest rate on central bank deposits below zero.

In such a scenario, those holding deposits would convert them to cash (which always yields 0%) which is better than a negative return from money on deposit. By removing cash, this escape route is blocked and a central bank can effectively move rates into negative territory.

In the words of *Fortune* magazine:

> If people are forced to keep their money electronically in bank accounts, banks could charge their customers for leaving their money unspent. In a paper currency world, rational actors would simply keep their money in cash if banks tried to institute negative interest rates.

Rogoff acknowledges that the elimination of paper currency would result in the loss of seigniorage for governments and the loss of anonymity for individuals. To this end, privacy advocates are concerned about who has access to the digital trail that is left by all our electronic purchases.

While the trend towards cashless payments is undeniable, I would not be counting them out of the economy just yet. Many people still believe that cash has virtues and are happy to keep using it. Also, never underestimate the power of habit and the sense of identity that comes from having a national currency.

A truly cashless global society will happen one day. But my sense is that day is still a long way off. To paraphrase Mark Twain, the news of the imminent demise of cash has been greatly exaggerated.

Posting Date: 4 April 2016

consumerconfidence

Economists examine lots of data to gauge the health of an economy and to gain a sense of where it is headed. Turn on the evening news and you'll be bamboozled by talk of exchange rates, bond yields, trade balances and current account deficits. But there is another way to take the temperature of an economy - consumer confidence.

Consumer confidence measures how you and I feel as consumers. Our feelings (or sentiments) about the economy are very important as they impact our willingness to spend, borrow and save. Every day consumers make financial decisions which individually seem insignificant. But when viewed collectively they provide a good barometer of a nation's economic well-being.

Consumer spending fuels most Western-based service economies and ranges between 50-75% of GDP for most nations. Consumer confidence indices, therefore, receive considerable coverage in the media because of the relationship between consumer confidence and household consumption growth.

Broadly speaking, when confidence is trending up, consumers spend and this contributes to a healthy economy. Conversely, when confidence is trending down, consumers tend to save more and spend less leading to a troubled economy. Consumer behaviour has the power to lead an economic recovery or drive an economic slowdown.

Consumer confidence is measured on a country by country basis - there is no single global measure. In each country, a random sample of consumers is surveyed on a periodic basis and asked attitudinal questions about the economy. In Australia, consumer sentiment is tracked via the weekly ANZ Bank/Roy Morgan survey of consumer confidence and the monthly Westpac Bank/Melbourne Institute consumer sentiment index.

Confidence surveys recognise that a consumer's state of mind is influenced by a combination of factors including economic news (petrol prices have risen), economic policy (the cash rate has fallen) and other economic lag indicators (job vacancies are steady). When factored with other macroeconomic variables (share market performance), the surveys produce a "score" which reveals whether people are optimistic or pessimistic about the future.

Of course, confidence is a strange thing - it has a habit of becoming a self-fulfilling prophecy. If we think we are going to have a downturn, our behaviour will likely produce that outcome. Emotions play a significant role in economic decisions and consumers who are fearful of the future (say, because of job uncertainty) will likely stop or reduce their spending.

The irony is that as people spend less, business activity slows and consumers may well find that their jobs are less secure. This self-defeating phenomenon is referred to by economists as the *paradox of thrift*. First articulated by John Maynard Keynes, this paradox describes the dilemma we face when times are tight (actual or perceived!).

During a downturn, we are encouraged to spend to keep the economy going. But our natural and understandable tendency is to save and this triggers a cause and effect spiral to decreased economic activity. The ride to recession begins when we all start saving our money and this reduces consumer spending. This, in turn, causes aggregate demand to fall and this, in turn again, results in a decline in total income.

When income falls, people have less to spend. As counter-intuitive as it sounds, individual savings (due to less spending) makes us collectively poor. While saving might appear beneficial at an individual level, it's actually detrimental to the population overall. One person's spending is another person's income. Thus, changes in consumer spending have a direct effect on the economy.

It is important to recognise that consumer sentiment also impacts whether or not consumers are comfortable in borrowing money. Economies are credit-driven which means households (and nations) invariably have to go into debt in order to grow. Post GFC consumers around the world have been paying down debt.

The crisis of confidence following the GFC caused consumers to become risk-averse. This saw the world enter a period of austerity and gave rise to the "cautious consumer". The cautious consumer remains with us as evidenced by higher household savings rates and deleveraging, both of which have become the "new normal" in many nations.

It's clear that we are not passive observers to what happens in the economy. Our collective decisions contribute to the economic trends we read about in the media. What households do at a micro level impacts the economy at a macro level through aggregate demand. The bottom line is that we help create the recessions and expansions that occur in the economy.

Posting Date: 18 May 2015

investment bonds

Virtually everyone borrows money at some stage of their life and the same holds true for businesses and governments. Just as households utilise finance to buy houses and pay for consumer durables, companies need funds to expand their operations and enter new markets while governments require money to provide infrastructure and other essential services.

Each sector of the economy taps different funding sources. Consumers can borrow money by taking out a personal loan or home loan. Corporations can raise working capital by using a combination of debt financing (bank loans and corporate bonds) and equity financing (issuing shares). Governments can raise money through taxes or by issuing bonds.

Every year, corporations and governments around the world issue trillions of dollars of bonds. Most bonds are known as fixed-income debt securities because the amount of income the bond generates annually is fixed when the bond is sold. The corporation or government entity promises to return the principal - the face value of the bond - on the specified maturity date.

Governments have historically issued specific-purpose bonds for the investing public. The vast highway system in the USA, the sewer networks of Paris and the World War II efforts of Britain were all financed by bonds. Fast forward to modern day Australia and the federal government is using infrastructure bonds to fund the bulk of the $43 billion National Broadband Network.

Corporate bonds, on the other hand, are debts issued by industrial, financial and service companies to finance capital investment. A debenture is an example of a corporate bond.

In Australia, bonds can be bought and sold on the share market via the ASX Interest Rate Market.

Bonds are essentially interest only loans and when you purchase a bond you become a "mini-banker", lending to a large corporate or government borrower. Bonds are also said to be similar to an I.O.U. - the issuer (e.g., corporation) must pay the interest due on the bonds whether or not it makes a profit. This is in contrast to dividends which are paid on shares at the directors' discretion.

The relationship between bond prices and interest rates is said to be inverse because bond prices and interest rates move in the opposite direction. When interest rates go up, bond prices go down and when interest rates go down, bond prices go up. At first glance, this inverse relationship appears illogical, but on closer examination it makes sense.

Let's say you buy a bond for $1,000 (par value). The bond pays interest at 5% per annum (coupon rate). The bond matures in four years (maturity date). This means you (the bondholder) will receive $50 interest per year. One year later you decide to sell your bond but market conditions have changed and interest rates have risen.

A bond offering $1,000 at maturity and a coupon rate of $50 per year is no longer attractive to investors. To lure potential buyers you must offer them an incentive in the form of a discount off the par value of your bond. This is because a $1,000 bond which matures in three years' time (same as your original bond) is now paying 6% or $60 per year.

An investor buying your bond today would only receive $150 in interest ($50 x 3). However, the same investor would receive $180 in interest ($60 x 3) in buying a newly issued bond. So, you sell your bond for $970 - a discount of $30. The investor now receives $150 in interest plus the additional $30 of principal when your bond matures.

Now that you understand the basics of bond pricing, let me introduce you to another technical term - yield. Yield is a figure that shows the return you get on a bond. In the above example, the bond with a 5% coupon and par value of $1,000 provides a yield of 5%. Nothing complex about that calculation.

But when the price goes down (below par) to $970 (a discount), the yield goes up to 5.15%. This happens because you are getting the same guaranteed return of $50 on an asset that is worth $970 ($50/$970). Conversely, if the bond goes up in price (above par) to $1030 (a premium), the yield shrinks to 4.85% ($50/$1030).

Although considered less exciting than shares, bonds play a critical role in our economy. Bondholders drive our economy and society to new heights. The next time you see a bridge being built or a production plant under construction, remember the vital role of bondholders and how their idle money is put to productive use.

Posting Date: 1 December 2014

shortselling

Imagine you are after a CD by your favourite band. A friend has the CD and agrees to lend it to you. You take the CD home and sell it on eBay for $25. You then buy another copy of the CD at a discount music outlet for $20. You give the replacement CD "back" to your friend and pocket the difference. You have just made $5 profit from what is known as short selling.

Selling something you don't own is counter-intuitive to most people but it happens every day on securities markets. When you sell short, you are betting the price of a stock will go down. It's the opposite of a long (normal) position, where you hope the value of a stock will go up. People sell stocks short when they think a stock is overvalued.

When an investor goes short, he must borrow stock from a broker and then sell those shares to a willing buyer. At some time the investor must buy back the same number of shares to cover his position as he originally sold borrowed stock and must return it to the owner by an agreed date.

If the price has dropped since the investor sold the stock, he can buy back the shares at the lower price thereby making a profit on the difference. If, however, the stock has risen in price, he must buy it back at the higher price and incur a loss.

Short selling is a perfectly legitimate means of hedging a portfolio. Indeed, it's seen by many as a valuable weapon in the day-to-day trading arsenal. But short selling is also a risky business as there's no guarantee that the price of a stock will go in the direction you want.

Betting on falling share prices is one way hedge funds generate profits, which is why they tend to do well when stocks perform poorly. This has led to accusations of stock price manipulation by some hedge funds, particularly where they are suspected of "bear raids".

In a typical bear raid, a trader "shorts" a target stock and then spreads bad news and/or false rumours about the target company to deliberately drive down the price. The trader profits between the original share price and the lower price that the share has been dragged down to as a result of the smear campaign.

While bear raids are illegal they do happen and during the Global Financial Crisis (GFC) this led a raft of people, including the Archbishops of Canterbury and York, to label short sellers as a renegade class of investors. In response to public outcry over short selling, the practice was temporarily banned or restricted in 17 countries during 2009. This gave rise to vigorous debate about the merits of short selling.

It is argued that if traditional fund managers can take punts on stocks going up (buying long), why can't hedge funds be allowed to take positions on stocks going down (selling short)? Put another way; is there really a difference between one investor selling her shares at a point where she thinks the price has peaked and another investor buying shares when he thinks they are overpriced?

Some see short selling - betting against companies - as an unscrupulous way of making money. In reality, short sellers are not villains as they identify overvalued companies and help restore more accurate prices. In doing this, they actually protect investors from buying stocks at prices higher than they should be.

For example, if traders had shorted Fannie Mae and Freddie Mac, there may never have been a GFC. Unfortunately, the activities of these two mortgage finance companies went unchecked. They bought billions of dollars of mortgages that were generated by homebuyers who bought houses at inflated prices. This created the housing bubble that led to the GFC.

Enron is another example of the benefits of short selling and how it can act as a first line of defence against financial fraud. Short sellers target companies based on their suspicion that something is not right (with the valuation) and this enabled them to spot fraud within Enron long before it became a scandal.

Lehman Brothers' demise is a further case where short sellers aided the market by shedding light on the company's true financial health. Following the GFC, research by a lecturer at the Australian School of Business found that short selling is actually good for the market.

I acknowledge that short sellers are not your stereotypical investors, but they do play an important role in protecting capital. Short sellers are sensitive to indicators of overvaluation and this helps them uncover problems, not create them. So care must be taken not to shoot the messenger. In the main, short sellers are market protectors, not market manipulators.

Posting Date: 13 July 2015

sub-zero rates

We all know that it makes no sense to keep your money under the mattress earning no interest. It's much better to put it in the bank so that it can generate a return. But that conventional wisdom is being challenged thanks to negative interest rates.

In parts of Europe and Japan, rates have moved into negative territory. As crazy as it sounds, depositors are actually being charged to keep their money in an account. It's an unorthodox tool being used by central banks to reinvigorate an economy when other options have been exhausted.

Central banks have long used monetary policy to stimulate an economy. Falling rates make borrowing more attractive and saving less attractive. Both of these factors act to boost consumer spending and business investment and this assists in kick-starting an economic recovery.

But there has long been a supposed barrier to how far rates can be cut - what economists call the *zero lower bound*. In simple terms, this means reducing rates below zero. Beyond this level, it is argued that people might be encouraged to take their savings out of the bank and hoard them in cash.

Physical cash carries an implicit rate of interest of 0%. This is a better return than paying for the privilege of putting money in a bank and earning a negative return. So, to escape the penalty of paying interest on their own money, depositors (so the theory goes) will flee for the safety of cash.

To date, negative rates have been quarantined to large depositors like financial institutions and major corporations. Central banks have imposed negative interest rates on their commercial banks, making it costly for those banks to store cash. The aim is to force the banks to lend out the cash, thus spurring the economy.

A recent article in *Global Post* explained it this way:

> It's normal practice in the banking world for commercial lenders to keep money with a central bank. One of the reasons they do that is to meet minimum reserve requirements - that's the percentage of customer deposits that the banks can't lend out and are usually kept with a central bank. The central bank normally pays interest on those holdings. Negative interest rates mean commercial banks are penalized for storing that extra cash with the central bank, instead of being paid positive, albeit very low, interest rates for loaning it out.

Adopting a negative interest rate setting is a bold move. Policymakers in Denmark, Sweden, Switzerland and Japan, as well as The European Central Bank, have all "turned negative". None, however, has achieved their goal of flushing cash out of the banking system to fuel inflation and growth through cheap credit.

According to Bank of America Merrill Lynch, the Negative Interest Rate Policy (NIRP) experiment is a failure. It noted that the aims of NIRP - to encourage borrowing and discourage upward pressure on currencies to boost trade - have not materialised.

With regard to currency values, the theory of the NIRP is that it causes a nation's currency to devalue. Negative rates encourage investors to search for better rates of return abroad, leading to less demand for a currency and therefore a fall in its value.

Devaluation makes a country's exports less expensive for foreigners and makes foreign products more expensive for domestic consumers. Raising the price of imports helps combat deflation while lowering the cost of exports enables a nation to offer its goods at more competitive prices.

Deflation occurs when consumers and businesses are reluctant to spend money. This leads to a collapse in demand for goods and services and results in a fall in prices, a slowdown in production and an increase in unemployment.

Such economic stagnation is typically addressed via what economists call a loose or expansionary monetary policy. In simple terms, this policy setting lowers rates - such as the NIRP - and is designed to stimulate lending and boost inflation.

The NIRP is a crisis policy that's taken the world into unchartered waters. It's never been tried before and it's prompting a rewrite of economic theories. Paying to save is counter-intuitive and it's too early to pass final judgment on its efficacy.

My sense is that over the longer term, negative rates will prove to be more of a problem than a solution.

Posting Date: 11 April 2016

financing infrastructure

Australians could not go about their daily lives without infrastructure. We need roads to get around, schools to educate our children, hospitals to care for the sick, electricity to power our homes, telecommunications networks to stay in touch, dams to provide us with drinking water and the list goes on.

A complex and interconnected series of networks and systems provide the infrastructure base of our nation. This infrastructure enables us to transport people and resources, produce and trade goods, provide essential services and drive economic growth.

Australia's need for infrastructure is constantly rising due to demographic changes and population growth. We all want less congested roads, more frequent and efficient trains, fewer flight delays due to inadequate airport facilities and better quality aged care.

More than four out of five Australians live in cities and there is currently a $500 billion backlog in sorely needed urban development including transport and energy. Australian governments at all levels are struggling to find the money necessary to clear this infrastructure backlog.

Australia's federal and state governments are understandably loath to levy the populace with higher taxes to pay for more government expenditure. They are also reluctant to increase debt levels, even though Australia has low levels of public debt compared to other OECD nations.

Alternate sources of funding must be found to finance the infrastructure required to underpin Australia's continued economic growth and social development. One solution is privatisation which can be used by governments to unlock funds for new infrastructure projects by selling existing public assets.

As I noted in a previous blog post, privatisation is alive and well in Australia and our burgeoning superannuation sector would like a bigger slice of the action. Ownership of government assets can be transferred to the community using superannuation funds that represent "mum and dad" owners.

An example of this occurred recently with the sale by the NSW Government of Port Botany and Port Kembla for $5.1 billion to a ports consortium. The consortium is made up of three Australian superannuation funds and a foreign owned infrastructure fund.

The symmetry between infrastructure investments and superannuation funds is touted as a match made in heaven. Superannuation seeks long-run, stable and strong returns which infrastructure assets provide. Given this, there is pent-up demand for infrastructure investment opportunities from superannuation funds.

Greenfield projects typically expose superannuation funds to construction, patronage and financial risks (e.g., toll roads). Selling off existing brownfield projects is a better way to raise funds. Thus, governments should build then privatise and then recycle capital for other projects.

Over the past two decades Australia's superannuation funds under management have grown from $140 billion to $1.4 trillion. Under current policy settings, the total pool of savings within the Australian superannuation market is expected to reach $3.2 trillion by 2022.

Australia's superannuation funds represent the fourth largest pool of investment funds in the world. Some of these funds can be invested in infrastructure - as a discrete investment class - as it offers certainty of income, inflation protection and less economic sensitivity.

Private financing of infrastructure by superannuation funds is not a new concept. Australia's superannuation industry is keen to undertake further investment in the domestic infrastructure sector. To facilitate this, governments must develop a strong pipeline of assets suitable for transfer to private ownership.

Selling off existing public assets to superannuation funds will provide a stable investment class to benefit superannuants while concurrently reducing Australia's infrastructure deficit. Better matching retirement savings and productive infrastructure is a win-win for everyone.

Posting Date: 3 June 2013

banking barometer

Banks and other financial institutions tend to mirror the markets in which they operate. More broadly, banking is a reflection of what's happening in an economy. Deposit growth, credit growth and asset quality all move in line with economic cycles i.e., periods of expansion and contraction.

When a national economy or region is characterised by optimism and growth, the demand for financing is high and this has a positive effect on a financial institution. Conversely, when the macroeconomic conditions are tough, banks reflect the troubles of a contracting economy including higher loan losses and lower credit growth.

The banking sector is a vital contributor to a country's economic growth. Indeed, it provides many of the key economic indicators which are used to measure the health of an economy. Interest rates and credit growth are two prime examples. Interest rates rise when an economy overheats and fall when an economy stalls.

Bank lending (credit growth) plays an important role in shaping the business cycle and the path of an economy. Economies are credit driven which is why the banking sector is often referred to as the lifeblood of an economy. Businesses, households and governments invariably have to go into debt in order to grow.

According to the US based Brookings Institution, the provision of credit "…fuels economic activity by allowing businesses to invest beyond their cash on hand, households to purchase homes without saving the entire cost in advance, and governments to smooth out their spending by mitigating the cyclical pattern of tax revenues and to invest in infrastructure projects".

Capitalism's most common single point of failure is the

interaction of real estate markets and finance. Almost all major events in modern economic history have been associated with a financial crisis. The most recent example is the Global Financial Crisis (GFC) which was precipitated by a credit bubble resulting from excessive leverage by subprime American households.

All economies are monetary which makes the financial sector and the real economy interdependent. A modern financial system allows commerce to flourish by providing the economic fuel that propels an economy forward. Moreover, an efficient and stable financial system is essential to enhance the prosperity of a nation's citizens.

At its core, the financial system allocates funds from savers to borrowers in an efficient manner. Banks and other financial institutions borrow from individuals, businesses and governments with surplus funds (savings). They then use those deposits (borrowed funds) to make loans to households, businesses and governments.

The process of taking in funds from a depositor and then lending them out to a borrower is known as financial intermediation. In Australia, banks, building societies and credit unions - known as Approved Deposit-taking Institutions (ADIs) - channel funds from people who have surplus money (savers) to those who lack the funds to undertake certain activities (borrowers).

Australia's ADIs provide valuable services to the rest of the economy. As I explained in a previous post, *Financial Sector*, the financial services industry touches the lives and wallets of virtually every Australian and contributes to our nation's well-being.

Following the GFC, the populace became disillusioned with the banking sector. Around the world, there was widespread anger that taxpayer funds were used to prop-up Wall Street.

Citizens were unhappy that they had to pay for the mistakes and oversights made by banks.

The public backlash to what many saw as rewarding bad behaviour is understandable. I too felt annoyed. However, that does not mean that finance is not good for us. Yale economics professor, Robert Shiller, argues this very point in his latest book, *Finance and the Good Society*.

To be clear, Professor Shiller is no apologist for the sins of the banking sector or the reckless behaviour that gave rise to the GFC. Indeed, Shiller was one of the earliest critics of our modern-day financial theory, which posits that financial markets are basically efficient. He predicted the housing bubble burst in the 2005 edition of his book, *Irrational Exuberance*.

Yet, in *Finance and the Good Society*, Shiller writes that "imperfect as our financial system is, I still find myself admiring it for what it does, and imagining how much more impressive it can be in the future". Shiller sees finance as a powerful tool for solving common problems and increasing the general well-being.

We all crave a better society and - notwithstanding its shortcomings - finance can help humanity achieve that goal.

Posting Date: 14 March 2016

personal debt

Last financial year there were 28,288 new bankruptcies in Australia. The overwhelming majority of these (90%) originated from voluntary debtor's petitions while only 10% were forced creditor's petitions. I think it's time we started talking about the increasing incidence of personal bankruptcy. Let's begin the discussion with an etymology lesson.

The word 'bankrupt' comes from the Italian, banca rotta, meaning 'broken bench'. In the sixteenth century, money lenders in Florence conducted their business on benches in outdoor markets where they exchanged money and bills. When a banker failed, his bench (aka "bank") was broken by the people as a mark of infamy and he was called a bankrupt.

During the first half of the 19th century, debtors' prisons were a common way to deal with unpaid debt in Europe. The father of English novelist, Charles Dickens, was imprisoned with his family in 1824 for a debt to a baker. Dickens later wrote about prison life in his masterpiece, *Little Dorrit*. The US also had debtors' prisons, but abolished them in the 1830s.

While the practice of publicly humiliating debtors no longer occurs, the propensity of people to get in over their heads has not changed. The mantra of some consumers today is: "I want it, I want it now and I'll borrow rather than save for the things I want." The end result for these individuals is often over-commitment and unsustainable household debt.

As I have previously opined, we have become a society of credit junkies. For many, materialistic expenditure is the drug of choice. Of course, there are those who would point the finger for rising personal indebtedness at over-eager banks and other lenders. But as I explained in an earlier post, this is too simplistic.

Despite advice to the contrary, many people deliberately pile on debt, typically racked up on several credit cards. These individuals often see bankruptcy as an easy and attractive option. Bankruptcy no longer has the social stigma it had in the past. It is now seen by many as a quick way of extinguishing debts in the mistaken belief that one's slate will be wiped clean.

Bankruptcy, however, should be an absolute last resort as the results are long lasting and far reaching. It can destroy an individual's credit rating and make it difficult for the person concerned to borrow again for some time. (Note: All prudent lenders would rather put in place a repayment plan rather than repossess a property or bankrupt a borrower.)

In fairness, some bankruptcies are caused by illness, divorce, a death in the family or redundancy. These largely uncontrollable events - "life's accidents" - should be viewed with compassion. In Australia, the number one trigger for bankruptcy is unemployment. Almost 40% of mortgage delinquencies are caused by injury and illness.

Bankruptcy laws have evolved over thousands of years and now protect debtors as well as creditors. But I believe the pendulum has swung too far. Some debtors are using bankruptcy as a modern day "get-out-of-jail-free" card. For my money, it's far too easy for Australians to declare bankruptcy.

It seems to me that both borrowers and lenders have a role to play in addressing the rising incidence of bankruptcy. Financial institutions need to do more to improve financial literacy skills and consumers need to become better money managers and live within their means.

If you've experienced a change in your personal circumstances and are struggling to keep up your mortgage payments, don't stick your head in the sand. Contact your lender and negotiate an affordable repayment arrangement. Don't wait until you are on a slippery slide to foreclosure or bankruptcy.

Posting Date: 2 November 2015

spending patterns

How you spend your money says a lot about you as a person. You may be an impulsive consumer who buys on the spur-of-the-moment or a wise owl who plans each purchase. Perhaps you are a spendthrift who requires regular retail therapy regardless of the cost or someone who is frugal and waits for sales and discounts.

We are all on a journey in the pursuit of happiness. Research reveals that materialistic gratification (like fashion) buys bursts of happiness which quickly wear off. New things are exciting only for a short while. Longer lasting happiness comes from buying experiences (like a family holiday). Shared experiences become ingrained and part of our long-term memory.

Another way of looking at expenditure is through the prism of wants and needs. You may want a fancy car, designer shoes and the latest electronic gadgets. But what you need is food on the table, clothes on your back and a roof over your head. Wants and needs vary from person to person and it's an individual choice as to how we spend our money.

Collectively, Australians spend billions of dollars annually on goods and services. In some cases, it's the thrill of the purchase that drives this expenditure while in others it represents the cost of essential living items. The cost of living is cited by many Australians as their number one source of anxiety, particularly those struggling to make ends meets.

According to the Australian Bureau of Statistics, half the money that Australian households spend on goods and services goes on housing, food and transport i.e., "essential" expenditure. Shelter is an essential human need and the price of having a place to call home is not cheap. For those renting or paying off a mortgage, housing costs are typically the largest area of household expenditure.

Housing affordability is a serious issue in Australia. We have one of the highest house price-to-income ratios in the world. The median multiple of house prices to household income in Australia is now 6.4 times, versus 4.7 in the UK and 3.6 in the US. Put another way, the median home in Australia costs 6.4 times as much as the median annual income.

Beyond our need for accommodation, we also need to feed ourselves and spending on food and non-alcoholic beverages accounts for the second largest portion of most household budgets. Of course, what we eat varies markedly from household to household. At an aggregate level, Australians spend four times more in supermarkets and grocery stores than in cafés and restaurants.

Almost 40% of all retail spending by Australian households finds its way into the coffers of our two supermarket giants - Coles and Woolworths. Every man, woman and child in Australia spends on average $100 a week at Coles and Woolworths or one of their related retail businesses. Woolworths claims that price is now the single most important driver of supermarket store choice for shoppers.

When it comes to transportation, Australians love cars. In 2012 there were more new cars purchased in Australia per capita than anywhere else in the world. According to the Australian Securities and Investment Commission, Australians spent $78.4 billion on their cars in 2012 and $2.2 billion on public transport.

Those households with money left over (referred to as discretionary income) after paying for the necessities of life are able to spend on "non-essential" goods and services. This includes things such as recreational activities, alcoholic drinks, personal care, sporting pursuits, fashion items, travel expenses, eating out, concert tickets, magazine subscriptions and yes, even mobile phones.

High levels of discretionary income in an economy are an indicator of prosperity and a high standard of living. It's also a measure of personal economic activity beyond subsistence. Discretionary income can be spent, saved or invested. Australians spend, on average, $960 per month on discretionary items.

Finally, Australians are creatures of habit when it comes to their spending habits. Research shows that 85% of us follow routine spending patterns. Moreover, two-thirds of Aussies never venture beyond a shortlist of favoured shops and almost half regularly visit the same shopping strip or mall. It seems that we do not cast a broad net when it comes to shopping.

Posting Date: 26 October 2015

savings rates

Isn't it strange how society often focuses on the plight of one group of people to the detriment of another? This phenomenon happens in all walks of life. Take health care for example. Prostate cancer kills more men in Australia each year than breast cancer kills women. Yet breast cancer receives more funding and more publicity than prostate cancer.

The disproportionate amount of time and money put into breast cancer research versus prostate cancer mirrors the disparity in media coverage and political sentiment towards borrowers and investors. When interest rates rise, every man and his dog laments the plight of those with a mortgage. Yet when rates fall, there is deafening silence regarding the resultant misery for self-funded retirees and savers.

Mortgage rates are a political hot potato, so mortgage holders receive lots of attention and sympathy when they go up. A hike in the cost of mortgages sours feelings towards the government of the day. Retailers, builders and other interest groups add fuel to the fire by blaming the Reserve Bank of Australia for their woes. Moreover, the media go into overdrive, whipping the mortgage belt into a frenzy as part of the interest rate blame game.

Contrast the above anger with the calm which greets an easing in rates. The tabloid press does not campaign on behalf of self-funded retirees for better term deposit rates. No powerful lobby group complains about the drop in the standard of living for older Australians. And the government is not moved to encourage banks to pass through, in full, rate rises on deposits to ease the cost of living pressures on seniors.

Falling rates may be a godsend to home owners, but they are not greeted with joy by those who rely on interest income. Over recent years, savers have experienced a cycle of "pay cuts" as the Reserve Bank has repeatedly slashed official interest rates.

But there has been little outpouring of pity for pensioners and savers reliant on cash to generate income.

It is instructive to note that two-thirds of Australians don't have a mortgage. So, falling rates benefit a smaller percentage of the population. On the other side of the coin, there are more savers than borrowers. Rising rates are a boon for a greater percentage of the population.

People on fixed incomes are not just feeling the pinch due to derisory interest rates but also because of inflation and taxation. This triple whammy means innocent savers are now struggling to find accounts that, after the taxman and inflation, offer a real rate of return. Slim pickings indeed and a bitter blow for savers who are understandably up in arms over their reduced spending power.

An increasing number of Australians live off investments and interest income. As more baby boomers retire over the next decade, a greater portion of society will become self-funded retirees and will welcome higher rates. Self-funded retirees were hit hard by the Global Financial Crisis. This group saw their superannuation capital plummet in the stock market downturn, yet they receive little support from government.

Many older Australians have worked hard and saved prudently to achieve self-sufficiency in retirement. They are responsible citizens who are to be applauded for standing on their own two feet. They are not a burden on the social security system as they reside outside the community of aged-pensioners requiring government assistance.

Next time interest rates fall, spare a thought for the hardship this creates for the senior members of our society. It's absolutely true that housing affordability and mortgage stress are real issues for younger Australians. But it's equally true that older Australians suffer in a low interest rate environment due to falling income streams.

Finally, it's important to remember that interest rates go down when times are tough and rise when the economy is going well. Who wants to continually live in tough economic conditions? Let the good times roll!

Posting Date: 15 June 2015

money management

We all have a relationship with money. For some, that relationship is healthy and fulfilling. For others, it is stressful and destructive. Money can be an empowering friend or a controlling enemy. It can give you power and status or it can cause heartache and misery.

Some of us are natural spenders while others are natural savers. Others still are money seekers who obsess over becoming wealthy. Regardless, money is not a panacea to all of life's problems. It does not buy happiness and having too much can bring its own set of problems.

Research reveals that life experiences (like a family holiday) give us more lasting pleasure than material things (like designer shoes). Yet people often deny themselves experiences (like the joy of giving) in favour of spoiling themselves with material goods.

To be sure, modern life is expensive which is why you need to differentiate between your wants and needs. We all need money to pay the rent and put food on the table. Beyond that, we need to live within our means and be careful not to take on "bad debt" to fund discretionary expenditure.

Money sparks many arguments. According to a US study, couples who argue about money early in their relationships - regardless of their income, debt or net worth - are at a greater risk for divorce. Arguments over money are typically more intense than other types of marital disagreements.

Some "experts" claim that men and women view money differently. It is said that men tend to take more financial risks while women typically see money as a security issue and are more risk-averse. In my experience, these are sweeping generalisations which do not reflect reality.

In lieu of drawing battle lines between the sexes over money, the focus should be on financial literacy for both genders. Money management skills are integral to a secure future and establishing good money habits - including personal and household budgeting - should begin in childhood.

There are many clichés about money - it makes the world go round, it doesn't grow on trees and it is the root of all evil. But for me, money is a reflection of our values. What you do with your money speaks volumes about the person you are and your priorities in life.

Some people choose a hedonistic, self-indulgent lifestyle while others have a totally different mindset to money based on abundance and generosity aligned to a higher purpose. Of course, how we choose to live our lives is up to us.

What is clear is that money is only a tool and we get to determine how we use it. Just review your last credit card statement to get a sense of what's important to you. Do the things you spend your money on bring you genuine joy and fulfilment or are you just trying to keep up with the Joneses?

The number of zeros after your bank balance is not a reflection of your self-worth. There are far greater riches in life than material wealth. Money is a means to an end, not an end in itself. This is why money is a distant second to happiness and health for most people.

Not even winning the lottery will make you happy forever. In fact, sudden wealth can be a curse. There are myriad examples of lottery winners whose lives became worse after winning truckloads of cash. Believe it or not, lottery winners are more likely to file for bankruptcy. Earned wealth brings more joy than unearned wealth.

Let me end with a tough question: If you had all the money in the world, what would you do with it?

Posting Date: 4 May 2015

capitalism's imperfections

It's been over four years since the Global Financial Crisis (GFC) reared its ugly head. Since that time a wave of GFC "aftershock" books has flooded the market. An assortment of academic economists, financial journalists and other experts have put pen to paper to explain why the world was brought to the brink of economic meltdown.

The post-crisis reading list is extensive and each author has a different take on the causes, consequences and lessons of the crisis. Many ask why we didn't see the economic collapse coming. The answer, according to University of Cambridge economist, Ha-Joon Chang, is simple: We didn't ask what they didn't tell us about capitalism.

In *23 Things They Don't Tell You About Capitalism*, Chang examines 23 aspects of capitalism he believes are misrepresentations or falsehoods. In highlighting these shortcomings Chang is careful to point out that his book is not an anti-capitalist manifesto. "Despite its problems and limitations, I believe that capitalism is still the best economic system that humanity has invented," he underscores.

Chang acknowledges that there's no real alternative to free-market capitalism describing it as "the worst economic system except for all the others". He says that "being critical of free-market ideology is not the same as being against capitalism". Rather, his aim is to tell "some essential truths about capitalism".

Popular economic wisdom suggests that markets should be free and interfered with as little as possible. In contrast, Chang argues that free-market policies have resulted in "slower growth, rising inequality and heightened instability in many countries".

He is critical of free-market ideology. "We have been told," says Chang, "that, if left alone, markets will produce the most efficient and just outcome." However, giving businesses maximum freedom and limiting government intervention was a contributing factor to the GFC.

To prevent another GFC, Chang believes we should ban complex financial instruments unless they can be shown to benefit society in the long run. He views today's financial markets as too efficient. They have produced so many new financial instruments that the sector has generated excess profits for itself in the short run while becoming a destructive force in the world. He writes:

> In the old days, when someone borrowed money from a bank and bought a house, the lending bank used to own the resulting financial product (mortgage) and that was that. However, financial innovations created mortgage-backed securities (MBSs), which bundle together up to several thousand mortgages. In turn, these MBSs ... were packed into a collateralized debt obligation (CDO). Then CDOs-squared were created by using other CDOs as collateral. And then CDOs-cubed were created by combining CDOs and CDOs-squared. Even higher-powered CDOs were created. Credit default swaps (CDSs) were created to protect you from default on the CDOs.

He goes on to make the obvious point that the same underlying assets (houses) were used again and again to derive new assets. This "financial alchemy" created an "increasingly tall structure of financial assets teetering on the same foundation of real assets". This, he explains, is akin to making an existing building taller without widening the base, thus increasing the chance of it toppling over.

Notwithstanding his criticism of the "overdevelopment of the financial sector", Chang does not believe that "all finance is a bad thing". Indeed, he acknowledges that financial development has been crucial in developing capitalism. However, when it comes to financial derivatives, Chang cites Warren Buffet's description of them as 'weapons of mass financial destruction'.

For anyone interested in a fascinating insight into the pitfalls of free-market capitalism, Chang's book is an easy and enlightening read. I found myself nodding in agreement most of the time. You too will discover that markets are not rational and business does not always know what is best. But I suspect you already knew that!

Posting Date: 29 October 2012

property prices

For most Australians, their home is their biggest asset, which is why tracking house prices runs deep in our national psyche. We all know our home is worth what someone is prepared to pay for it. Beyond that, the law of supply and demand explains how buyers and sellers interact to determine property prices.

The main determinants of the demand for housing are demographic and economic factors such as income level, employment rate, consumer confidence, population growth, net migration and household formation. Housing supply, on the other hand, is the stock of houses available for sale and includes both new homes and existing dwellings.

The supply and demand equation for housing see-saws and there is invariably a gap between the two. Sometimes it's a seller's market (demand exceeds supply) while at other times it's a buyer's market (supply exceeds demand). Over and above this, house prices go in cycles creating booms and busts.

There is much debate about who is to blame for housing booms. Some cite monetary policy (rates too low), others point the finger at government ineptness (inadequate land supply) while others vent at real estate agents (talk market up). Not to be forgotten as a contributing factor is the "irrational exuberance" of borrowers.

An often repeated mantra in Australia is that we don't have enough houses to cater for our immigration-fuelled population growth. The popular assertion is that while migration over the past decade has been very high, we are not building any more dwellings today than we did 20 years ago. The reality is that Australia's alleged housing shortage is nowhere near as bad as claimed.

What is true is that Australian house prices are the second

most expensive in the world. Relative to our incomes, we Aussies have to fork out more than any other nationality to buy a home - 6.4 times average annual household income. This compares to a house price to household income ratio of 3.6 in the US and 4.7 in the UK.

The problem of home affordability in Australia has become acute for many people on low and moderate incomes. Housing affordability relates to a person's ability to pay for their housing. Standard affordability measures reflect the interaction of two factors: the mortgage interest rate and the ratio of housing prices to household incomes.

Spiralling real estate prices, particularly in Sydney over recent years, have made the situation worse, even with record low interest rates. Housing price increases have outpaced rises in incomes. Home ownership for many young Australians now seems an illusory goal. Foreign buyers and property investors are said to be making the situation worse.

In 1970, according to the National Centre for Social and Economic Modelling, Australia had average house prices of about $12,500 - about three times the typical income. Now, nationally, we have average house prices of $420,000 - about six-and-a-half times the average income. In Sydney, the typical house price is about nine times the median household income.

For baby boomers, home ownership was the great Australian dream. For Gen Yers, gaining a foothold in the property market is proving to be the great Australian nightmare. A serious social problem indeed and one that is likely to get worse with Australia's population, according to the latest Treasury Intergenerational Report, predicted to reach 39.7 million by 2055.

Posting Date: 9 June 2015

aussie dollar

A big surprise over recent years has been the strength of the Australian dollar. As we rode the biggest resources boom in our nation's history, commodity prices rose strongly and this helped propel our currency to new heights. In June 2012, the Aussie dollar reached and then passed parity with the greenback.

Currencies, like any commodity, are subject to the free market forces of supply and demand. A currency will tend to become more valuable whenever demand for it is greater than the available supply. It follows, therefore, that when a country imports goods, it decreases the value of its domestic currency while exports increase a currency's value.

While the activities of governments and corporations impact currency prices, you and I also influence exchange rates as domestic consumers, international travellers and global investors. When you buy an imported car from Japan, convert dollars to Euros while travelling through Europe or invest superannuation savings in US equities, you settle these transactions by supplying Australian dollars.

The demand for our currency, on the other hand, is driven by those who have foreign currency and want to buy Australian dollars such as in-bound tourists and foreigners purchasing our exports. As I noted in an earlier post, *International trade*, people in other countries are eating our beef, drinking our wine, using our software and riding in our fast ferries thanks to our exports.

The Aussie dollar is one of the most traded currencies in the world. As our exports largely comprise raw materials, the Aussie dollar is referred to as a commodity currency. The direction of our currency depends on Australia's conditions/prospects and includes demand factors such as economic outlook, political stability, interest rates and the level of inflation.

Australia enjoys significant foreign investment as overseas investors have confidence in our local economy. The perceived risk of investing here is low and this influences the volume of capital inflow. An important consideration for investors is the level of real interest rates relative to those in other countries.

Following the Global Financial Crisis (GFC), Australia had the highest interest rates in the developed world and this attracted overseas money. International investors pushed up the demand for our local currency. For a while, the Australian dollar was one of the best performing currencies in the world.

When the dollar rises sharply it hurts our export industries such as manufacturing, tourism, agriculture and higher-education. This is why, *inter alia*, the Reserve Bank of Australia (RBA) has been lowering the cash rate in the hope of bolstering economic growth in these and other sectors. Following the latest cash rate reduction in May, the RBA said:

> The Australian dollar has declined noticeably against a rising US dollar over the past year, though less so against a basket of currencies. Further depreciation seems both likely and necessary, particularly given the significant declines in key commodity prices.

Put another way, the RBA was saying that a lower exchange rate was necessary to achieve balanced growth in the economy as the Australian dollar was - at that stage - considered to be overvalued. Policymakers have been steadfast in their determination to drive down the dollar (which the RBA believes should be below US75¢) and it now sits at US69¢.

The central bank's efforts to engineer depreciation in our currency - to help grow export volumes by boosting global competitiveness - are laudable. However, much to the frustration of the RBA, many forces impact exchange rates - not just interest rates - and no country can control the ups and downs.

Posting Date: 7 September 2015

debt bogeyman

Australia is a world leader in low government debt and our economy is the envy of most other countries. Yet as one prominent economist has pointed out, Australia's debt phobia is in full force. At a time when the economy needs every single cent to support an increasingly uncertain economic environment, there have been emotive calls for budget frugality.

The debt bogeyman is alive and well even though we have a AAA credit rating, low public debt as a proportion of GDP and a low yield on Australian government bonds (the interest rate we pay on our debt). Note, if we had too much debt, yields would be higher as was the case with Italy and Spain post-GFC when both nations had unsustainable debt.

It is interesting to note that around 75% of Australia's $257 billion stock of Commonwealth Government Bonds is held by foreigners including central banks and sovereign wealth funds. These institutional investors hold our bonds (securities) as they are a low-risk, long-term, safe-haven investment option. They are certainly not seen as junk bonds!

As I pointed out in an earlier post, *In defence of deficits*, it is a sweeping generalisation to say that debt is inherently bad. Economies are credit-driven which means nations and households invariably have to go into debt in order to grow. Used wisely and prudently, debt at both a household and sovereign level should not evoke feelings of gloom and doom.

In a later post, *Budget surplus not imperative*, I challenged the notion that a budget surplus is always preferable to a budget deficit. In reality, there are bad surpluses and good deficits. A bad surplus runs down services to the public by reining in public finances too hard. A good deficit, on the other hand, borrows to fund investments in productive infrastructure.

In a further post again, *The media politician and deficit hysteria*, I argued that opinion poll driven politicians often sacrifice long-term economic credibility for short-term populist reforms. The electorate has been conditioned to believe that debt is bad, so any political leader who does not pledge to lower our national debt is seen to be unworthy of our vote.

Our obsession in Australia with national public debt is self-defeating and gives rise to policies which are against our own self-interest. Right now we should be making prudent investments in infrastructure. But the very people who scream about poor roads and overcrowded hospitals are the same who protest against more government borrowing to fund vital public resources.

Infrastructure is critical to Australia's long-term growth and prosperity. As I revealed in *Financing infrastructure*, there is currently a $500 billion backlog in sorely needed urban development including transport and energy. Australian governments at all levels are struggling to find the money necessary to clear this infrastructure backlog.

Governments can raise money through taxes or by issuing bonds. The Federal Government will continue to raise money by issuing bonds, but it also needs to raise taxes. While we don't have a debt problem we do have a taxation problem. Our current tax structure is fiscally unsustainable and you and I will be asked to pay more - it's just a matter of time.

As I explained in *A fairer tax system*, taxes need to rise to cover increased public spending for a growing and aging population. We need more schools, more hospitals, more roads and the list goes on. Without an increase in government receipts we are setting ourselves up for permanent structural deficits.

At the end of the day, it is a myth to say that debt alone is an indicator of sound economic management. Governments are not about profit and loss, which is why the ultimate objective of fiscal policy is not balancing the budget. At this stage of our economic cycle, I'm okay with the budget being in the red. Remember, if debt was truly bad no one would borrow to buy a house!

Posting Date: 3 February 2014

housing data

The Australian housing sector is the nation's largest and arguably most important asset class. According to a recent RP Data Property Report, the total value of homes across the country as at December 2011 was $4.54 trillion. Australian equities, by way of comparison, had a total market capitalisation at the same time of $1.17 trillion.

Australia's love affair with property is well known. More than 60% of all Australians own a home - one of the highest rates of home ownership in the world. The Reserve Bank of Australia estimates that around 6% of the housing stock, or 500,000 dwellings, changes ownership each year.

While home ownership remains the great Australian dream, over the past decade there has been a decline in the number of first home buyers climbing on the property ladder. Australian Bureau of Statistics data shows that young adults are remaining in the parental home for longer periods. Some claim that Generation Y may never own a home due to declining affordability.

In the eighth International Housing Affordability Survey released in January it was noted that "Australia exhibited the worst housing affordability of any national market outside Hong Kong". The unaffordability ratio is derived by dividing the median house price by the median household income.

The Survey considers a median multiple rating of three times or under to be "affordable". Housing markets with a median multiple of 3.1 to 4 times are labelled "moderately unaffordable". The ratio of 4.1 to 5 times is "seriously unaffordable" while "severely unaffordable" markets have ratios of 5.1 times or above.

The median-priced house in Australia's major cities was an average of 6.7 times the median household income. Within

Australia, Sydney easily retained first place as the most unaffordable city, with the median house price 9.2 times median household income.

The fall in home ownership among Australians less than 35 years is typically attributed to diminishing affordability and delays in family formation. If current home ownership trends continue, Australia's largest industry superannuation fund claims that one in four Australian retirees will be renters rather than home owners by 2040.

Finally, no discussion about housing would be complete without mention of the old chestnut - whether housing is a productive or unproductive investment. Some economists regard housing as an unproductive form of investment relative to industrial investment. The broad arguments go something like this.

Putting capital at risk for a future return lies at the heart of capitalism. Investing in machines in a factory which creates jobs and pays taxes is an example of productive capital at work. Conversely, assets that sit idle are unproductive. Ergo, an investment in real estate which merely changes ownership of existing wealth and does not produce new wealth is an unproductive asset class.

There's no doubt that investments in new factories and basic infrastructure like roads benefit society. But investment in property also contributes to the economy by creating an array of jobs directly and indirectly associated with constructing, renovating and maintaining homes. This workforce also pays truckloads of taxes.

Housing is a macroeconomic issue. The housing sector accounts for a significant proportion of national economic activity/investment and exerts an important influence on other economic factors including national capital, household wealth and household debt.

As noted by Australian economist, Christopher Joye, shelter - along with food and security - is among the most basic of human needs. Secure and affordable housing is central to our standard of living and way of life. A place to call home - how does one put an economic value on that?

Posting Date: 23 April 2012

new year

Well hello again! It's good to be back online. I was starting to get twitchy from my self-imposed break from the blogosphere. Taking a short time-out from the rigours of weekly posts has enabled me to recharge my batteries. I look forward to sharing my thoughts with you on a variety of business related topics during 2013.

I trust you had a wonderful Christmas/New Year period. Australians have a strong affinity with summer and a hearty appetite for the outdoors. The weather has been perfect for fish and chips on the beach, a barbie in the backyard or a concert in the park. Summer is in full swing so there's still time to attend an open air movie or take a dip in the ocean.

It's also the time to set some goals. At the stroke of midnight, many people welcomed the New Year with a list of resolutions. Apparently, the two most common resolutions are to lose weight and shed debt. Next on the list of New Year goals is to spend more time with family and friends. The desire to learn something new and to take a trip also features on many to do lists.

All of us need to periodically evaluate our lives and many believe the beginning of a New Year is a good time to do that. However, research shows that the majority of people fail in their annual attempt to start afresh and turn over a new leaf. With the best of intentions, many set too many goals and/or are not prepared to follow through with tangible actions (eg, start exercising).

Personally, I do not wait for the New Year to establish goals. "Why put off until tomorrow what you can do today" is my motto. Regardless of when you set goals, achieving them requires more than just good intentions - you need an implementation plan. Without a roadmap, you invariably end up spinning wheels and never move from goal setting to goal accomplishment.

The same holds true in the corporate world where just wanting something is not enough. Yet many companies write a business plan and then metaphorically (and sometimes, literally) leave it sitting on the shelf to collect dust. Consequently, 70% of strategic plans are never successfully implemented as organisations do not move from thinking to doing.

The acid test for any strategic plan is the degree to which it impacts the daily activities and behaviours of the members of an organisation. To this end, if you say you want to improve your service, you need to change your operational and innovation processes. In the same way, if you say you want to get fit, you invariably need to change your eating and exercise habits.

Academics define a strategic plan as "a program of planned change". So, to be successful, you must be able to manage change and that is something we do well at Gateway Credit Union. We are in a state of constant change as the needs of our members are always changing. We never procrastinate and have disciplines in place to ensure the rubber quickly hits the road in terms of implementation.

Thomas Edison famously said that "vision without execution is hallucination". Edison valued not only idea generation but also implementation. So did Steve Jobs and Bill Gates who both knew how to connect vision to execution and so must you to achieve your goals. Remember, a vision without a plan is merely a pipe dream.

Have a great 2013 and I hope all your dreams - sorry, I meant to say goals - come true!

Posting Date: 21 January 2013

household budget

Marriages and mortgages have something in common - they are both "death pledges". In a non-secular marriage ceremony each partner vows to stay with the other "until death do us part". Home buyers who execute a mortgage also commit to a "death pledge", but not in a literal sense. To explain this, we need to take a brief diversion for a quick history lesson.

Most of the English language has its roots in other languages, with many words derived from Germanic languages. Much of the English vocabulary has also been acquired from Latin, in many cases by way of French. A good example of this etymology is the word mortgage.

Mortgage is made up from two words - 'mort' and 'gage'. Mort (meaning death) comes from the Latin word mortuus from which we get mortuary and mortal. Gage (meaning pledge) comes from the old French and means a 'hold or grip' over something of value to ensure the payment of a debt.

So, a mortgage is a death pledge and this can be viewed from two perspectives. If the borrower repays the loan, the property becomes "dead" to the lender and the mortgage document is annulled. Conversely, if the borrower defaults, the property is forfeited and becomes "dead" to the borrower.

Fast forward to present time and couples want their mortgage "dead" (discharged) to improve the financial equity in their relationship. Research shows that couples fight about money twice as much as they fight about sex. In fact, money is typically cited as the number one cause of marriage break ups.

While love may bind us together, money can wrench us apart. Most families have some level of debt and this is often the root cause of much of the stress and arguments in households. Tough economic times further strain wallets and relationships.

It's said that opposites attract, but when a spender marries a saver, financial feuds are inevitable. The saver can be seen as a tightwad while the spender is viewed as a squanderer. "Her" shopping sprees and "his" sports toys can create battle lines.

But financial harmony is possible in a union that is for richer, for poorer. Openly talking about money is a good start. A couple will never truly live happily ever after if they don't work out differences over finances. Money provides safety and security, so any plan must cover both financial and emotional needs.

At a minimum, you need to agree a household budget and set some financial goals. Beyond that, there is no one right way to manage household finances - it's up to you. You must, however, understand each other's financial expectations and try to accommodate the needs of both parties.

Money will always be a hot topic for any couple and shared financial bliss often involves compromises. Some simple give-and-take can move you closer to being on the same financial page. The key is to allow views and opinions to be shared in an atmosphere of mutual trust and respect.

Posting Date: 8 July 2013

quantitative easing

If you're a baby boomer or older, you'll recall the TV ads from the 1970s for the non-alcoholic drink, Claytons. It was marketed as "the drink you have when you're not having a drink". Quantitative easing (QE) is like Claytons' money - the money you manufacture without actually printing it.

QE enables a country to create new sums of money out of thin air. Central banks have the power to wave a magic QE wand and produce money electronically. There's no need to crank up the printing presses and put crisp new bills into circulation.

The conjuring-money-out-of-thin-air trick is quite easy. The magician must be a central bank (e.g., Bank of England) and it simply uses a computer to transfer funds to itself. It doesn't even have to say "abracadabra"!

If you look under the magician's cape, you'll see that QE is a monetary policy weapon. In the war against recession, central banks have been cutting rates (i.e., easing monetary policy) to revive ailing economies by making it cheaper for people to borrow.

But having reduced official interest rates to close to zero, the US and the UK central banks have effectively run out of ammunition. While they can't make money cheaper, they can make it more plentiful. So they've decided to directly inject more money into the economy via a non-traditional weapon - QE.

QE involves a central bank buying up assets - government and corporate bonds - with money it electronically creates from new central bank reserves. The financial institutions selling the assets have the "new" money deposited into their accounts which boosts the money supply.

The theory is that banks will use the additional funds to lend to customers thereby stimulating demand and improving the health of the economy. There is debate among economists as to whether QE will be effective. The pros and cons of the debate can be technical.

While there's no guarantee that QE will work, many economists are optimistic it will do the trick. As AMP Chief Economist, Shane Oliver, pointed out in a recent market update, Australia has no need to engage in QE. For now, we'll just sit on the sidelines and watch the magic show.

Posting Date: 15 June 2009

banking jargon

My wife is a nurse by training. She can tell you that *gluteus maximus* is the medical term used to describe the muscles in your buttocks whereas I thought it was somehow related to the Roman General, Maximus Meridius, played by Russell Crowe in the movie *Gladiator*. (Yep, I'm a butt head!)

Just as my wife is comfortable with medical lingo, I'm used to financial terminology. It can be very confusing when you are an outsider to an industry that has its own lexicon. It's no surprise, therefore, that the average punter is struggling to understand the credit crisis - it has challenged the financial literacy of even astute investors!

Be honest, had you heard of *quantitative easing* twelve months ago? How about *short selling*? What about exotically named instruments like *Collateralized Debt Obligations*, *Credit Default Swaps* and *Floating Rate Notes*? Do your eyes glaze over when you see terms like *toxic assets* and *margin loans*. And what do you make of the comical names of *Freddie Mac* and *Fannie Mae*?

This doubletalk is hard to swallow and causes the best of us to experience a system meltdown. We all deserve a *fiscal stimulus* to ease our household *budget deficits* caused by falling *aggregate demand*. Little wonder *consumer confidence* has plummeted.

We also need to be shielded from the *bears* and *bulls* which roam the markets. And what about all the "isms" we have to put up with? These describe the various schools of economic thought and include *socialism*, *capitalism*, *monetarism* and *protectionism*.

If you haven't fallen into a trance yet you could turn to a friend to help you decipher this economic jargon. But don't ask economic luminaries Milton Friedman, John Maynard

Keynes or Adam Smith. Firstly, they're all dead and secondly their modern day followers will give you differing explanations of the current crisis.

Well, I should wind up now and *bailout* before the *AAA rating* on my *blue chip* blog is downgraded and I'm unable to *hedge* against a *dead cat bounce* in readership which will yield a *subprime* outcome.

Posting Date: 9 June 2009

margin loans

The rising tide of margin lending has swept many Australians off their feet. Prior to the credit crisis, using debt to fund share market investments seemed a good idea. But the worst bear market in Australia's history has delivered a tough lesson - margin loans don't cope with a sudden downturn in stock markets.

Dipping one's toe in the water before diving in head first is always good advice for any novice. Yet many investors failed to follow the maxim: Look before you leap. Worse still, some of those who did rely on expert advice were ill-informed of the pitfalls associated with margin lending.

It's now clear that the general populace was not ready for a product that was previously the domain of high-net-worth, sophisticated investors. Leveraged trading is not for everyone as clients of Storm Financial Services have painfully discovered. Even some bull market high flyers have been severely hurt by margin loans.

Australian investors are now showing understandable caution to margin loans, but used sensibly they remain a useful investment strategy. The Federal Government recently foreshadowed the introduction of new regulatory measures for margin lending to protect investors.

While gearing to invest can ramp up your returns, make sure you understand the risks. Speculators forced to stump up money to meet a margin call have learnt a costly lesson - always leave an adequate margin of safety otherwise your nervous bank may call in your loan. If you can't raise enough cash to top up the security on your margin loan, your lender will simply sell your stock.

It pays to take a more conservative approach and borrow less than the maximum loan-to-value ratio (LVR). A lower gearing level gives you a buffer if the value of your investment falls. And never forget the golden rule - *caveat emptor!*

Posting Date: 23 February 2009

money history

One way to make sense of the present financial crisis is to look back at the past. That's exactly what Harvard University professor, Niall Ferguson, does in his book, *The Ascent of Money: A Financial History of the World*.

I recently read Ferguson's tome and enjoyed it. While the book has received mixed reviews, I believe it's well worth a read. Ferguson charts the rise of money over the past 5,000 years - from the clay tokens of ancient Mesopotamia to the bits and bytes of today's electronic money.

The core lesson which arises from the history of money and finance is that every bubble bursts. As Ferguson notes: "Sooner or later the bearish sellers outnumber the bullish buyers. Sooner or later greed turns to fear." *The Ascent of Money* shows the current financial dislocation is just another crisis among the many that have struck the financial world throughout its history.

"Money," according to Ferguson, "amplifies our tendency to overreact, to swing from exuberance when things are going well to deep depression when they go wrong. Booms and busts are products, at root, of our emotional volatility."

Ferguson argues that money has fuelled human progress and that the finance industry is the essential backdrop behind all history. "The ascent of money has been essential to the ascent of man." Ferguson also believes that "the evolution of credit and debit was as important as any technological innovation in the rise of civilization".

He goes on to say that behind each great historical phenomenon lies a financial secret. For example: "It was Nathan Rothschild as much as the Duke of Wellington who defeated Napoleon at Waterloo." Ferguson reveals why English speaking people developed their obsession with buying and selling homes and explains how finance evolves through natural selection.

He also documents how a new financial revolution is propelling China from poverty to wealth in the space of a single generation - an economic transformation unprecedented in human history. I'll have more to say about that in my blog post next Monday.

Posting Date: 26 June 2009

economic quiz

Spaghetti originated in China, not Italy. Tulips are native to Turkey, not Holland. Nikola Tesla invented the radio, not Marconi. The sun is actually white, not yellow. The question that arises from this quick quiz is somewhat confronting: Do we really know what we think we know?

The average Joe "knows" that economics deals with the production and consumption of goods and services. However, economics is really about how we make decisions. It's a body of knowledge that explains how we make choices. Given our limited resources and unlimited wants (referred to by economists as scarcity) how do we make tradeoffs between alternatives?

As consumers we make choices every day. Should I buy that new car? Or should I extend my house instead? Maybe I should just take the family for a holiday? Or how about I put the money aside for a rainy day?

Our collective decisions contribute to the economic trends we read about in the media. We help create the recessions and expansions that occur in the economy. The latest economic statistics tell us that we are not a happy lot. Australia now has the second lowest level of consumer confidence in the OECD but the Reserve Bank of Australia says the fall is not disastrous.

What is not debatable is that we have tightened our belts. We are spending less on eating out. We are buying fewer magazines. We are purchasing fewer new cars. And we are building fewer homes. In America, changed consumer spending patterns has caused leading economist, David Rosenberg, to suggest that "frugality is now replacing frivolity".

With restaurant meals off the menu, big ticket expenditure

on hold and petrol prices rising, people are understandably worried. But history shows that things will get better. Consumer sentiment will bounce back. The good times will return. It's all part of the (financial) circle of life.

Posting Date: 22 September 2008

economic stimulus

On 8 December 2008 the Rudd Government will pump $10.4 billion into the pockets of Australian consumers. The cash transfer to low and middle income earners as well as pensioners and first home buyers should reduce the risk of a recession - assuming the recipients don't hoard it!

The fiscal stimulus package represents a modern day New Deal and is based on Keynesian economics. The British economist, John Maynard Keynes, believed that in a downturn, fiscal policy should be used to stimulate the economy.

As a result of the Global Financial Crisis (GFC) governments around the world are moving to shore up confidence but this does not mean that, longer term, free markets are out and governments are back in business. The health of our economy (and others) is declining and, in Australia's case, I believe a pre-Christmas injection of cash is just what the doctor ordered.

What the academic heavyweight of laissez-fair capitalism, Professor Milton Friedman, would make of this is probably not hard to guess. Friedman was a staunch advocate of monetarism and argued that government action was at the root of inflation.

In line with the underlying sentiment I espoused in a recent post, I am of the school which believes that, right now, we need a Keynesian recession buster. I believe the government's economic stimulus package will help the economy stay alive in the short term and that a hit of Keynes will do us good.

Lest there be any confusion, I am neither a Keynesian purist nor a monetarist purist. One has to be pragmatic and Keynes is undergoing an understandable revival in the face of unprecedented market conditions. In normal times, I believe that governments should play a much smaller role in the economy and that we need to be cautious of over regulation.

Posting Date: 24 November 2008

powershift

When historians talk about turning points in history there is always debate about which events should be included. Major wars, natural disasters, scientific revolutions and social upheavals always feature in the list of decisive moments that have changed our world. However, single events - even the most dramatic - often prove less important in the long run in shaping history.

The true watersheds in human history often go unnoticed initially. Unlike the dropping of an atomic bomb or the landing of a man on the moon, major transformational changes occur subtly and their effects emerge slowly. Such is the case with economic change.

In 1889 John Hay, the (then) US Secretary of State, said: "The Mediterranean is the ocean of the past, the Atlantic the ocean of the present and the Pacific the ocean of the future." In the early 1990s futurist, John Naisbitt, identified "The Rise of the (Asia) Pacific Rim" as one of 10 MegaTrends for the new millennium. Both of these prophecies are now reality.

The rise of the Asian Tigers, the emergence of China as an economic powerhouse, the restoration of Japan's growth and the momentum of India will see Asia become the dominant economic region in the world. The growing influence of Asia as a world economic power is undeniable.

Most commentators agree that the 21st century will see Asian countries take over as market leaders. While no one is suggesting the total demise of the West or that Asian nations will become absolute masters of the universe, a power shift is occurring.

A detailed explanation of this shift can be found in the book - *The New Asian Hemisphere: The Irresistible Shift of Global*

Power to the East. It's about time that world leaders started embracing this new reality. Perhaps the next G20 meeting should be held in Jakarta or Seoul and not Washington.

Posting Date: 6 July 2009

savingscrisis

Many Australians find it difficult to save. As a nation, we are among the worst savers in the developed world. Nearly 40% of working Australians do not have enough savings to last them more than one month if they lost their job.

Banks and other authorised deposit-taking institutions (ADIs) convert household savings into loans for other households wishing to finance the purchase of a home. Demand for home finance, however, exceeds the supply of deposits as Australians borrow more than they save.

To fund this imbalance our banks and other lenders borrow money offshore to lend for domestic purposes. This creates a reliance on global capital markets and a resultant exposure to credit market price changes as occurred during the Global Financial Crisis (GFC).

Our household saving - the difference between household disposable income and household consumption - has declined over the last three decades. In fiscal 2003 it became negative and remains so. Due to easy access to consumer credit (e.g., credit cards, home equity loans) households have seen less reason to save for emergencies.

Also, Australia is currently in her 19th year of uninterrupted economic expansion and households tend to save less in the good times and put more away when the outlook is less promising. Which is why the saving ratio is viewed as a barometer of the overall state of the economy.

But higher saving ratios are not of unlimited benefit as they come at the cost of lower consumption ratios. Too much saving translates directly into too little consumer demand. This is what occurred during the GFC when many households stopped spending, creating a *paradox of thrift*.

To an economist, saving is the decision to defer consumption and to store this deferred consumption in some form of asset. Savings are one of the most heavily taxed forms of assets under the current tax system and this discourages savings. Maybe the yet-to-be-released Henry Review will address this?

One of the concerns behind the introduction of compulsory superannuation in 1986 was the decline of the household saving rate in Australia. Superannuation has forced us to save for retirement but has not changed the "voluntary" saving ratio.

The end result is that we are generating insufficient savings to fund the investment needed to build our great nation. We have become dependent on foreign savings making us a debtor nation. A large part of our current account deficit comprises the interest on the money we borrow from abroad.

Australian households need to move from conspicuous consumption to inconspicuous saving. You can do your bit by tucking away some money each pay day for a rainy day.

Posting Date: 22 February 2010

interest rates

Why is the sky blue? Why does hair turn grey? Why do boomerangs come back? Sometimes simple questions are hard to answer, and so it is with money matters. Why does the world have debt? Why is there economic inequality? Why do interest rates rise and fall? Today, let's have a go at answering that final question.

It helps to think of money as a product, with interest rates being the cost of that product. Like all products, the price of money is determined by the economic "law" of supply and demand. Rising interest rates are a function of a high demand for money against a low supply of currency. Conversely, falling interest rates are a signal of weak loan demand alongside high money supply.

When the economy performs well and confidence is high, people are more likely to take out loans and this can push interest rates higher. Alternatively, when the economy is in recession and confidence is low, loan demand is weak and banks lower interest rates in order to compete for limited business.

It can be seen that the performance of the Australian economy affects the demand for money and this is where the Reserve Bank of Australia (RBA) steps in. The RBA influences the amount of money flowing into the nation's financial system by raising and lowering interest rates, similar to turning water on and off like a faucet - hence the term liquidity.

There are a range of factors that affect interest rates such as inflation, the strength of the dollar and the pace of economic growth. The central bank in each country can cause the interest rate for their currency to rise and fall. Inflation is probably the main reason why interest rates move up and down.

When people spend strongly, prices increase which causes inflation to rise. Conversely, when consumers don't have money to spend, prices and inflation ease or stay steady. In techno-speak, spending by households (consumption) contributes significantly to aggregate demand which, in turn, fuels inflation.

That's why households get caught in the crossfire in the war against inflation. Whenever the RBA tightens monetary policy to dampen demand (restrain expenditure) interest rates rise. Such rises do not discriminate between rich and poor households which is why monetary policy is referred to as a blunt instrument.

Each month the RBA meets to consider whether it should change the official overnight Cash Target Rate (CTR). The CTR is the rate at which the RBA lends to financial institutions. This interest rate then affects the whole range of interest rates set by banks, building societies and credit unions for their own savers and borrowers.

The RBA sets the official cash rate with the goal of controlling inflation, while banks and other financial institutions set interest rates to make a profit. As outlined above, households also influence interest rates through their spending and savings habits. Interest rates are increased to moderate consumer demand and inflation and reduced to stimulate demand.

Discussing the link between consumer demand and inflation is like wondering which came first, the chicken or the egg. They are cause and effect - all part of a cycle that is monitored by the RBA. Indeed, changes in consumer spending have an important effect on the path of the economic cycle.

The bottom line is that you are not a passive observer to interest rate movements. What your household does at a micro level impacts interest rates at a macro level through aggregate demand.

Posting Date: 16 April 2012

moneysupply

The currency you have in your wallet or purse has no intrinsic value in and of itself. Bank notes are just colourful pieces of paper with ink patterns used to represent different denominations. But paper money has implicit monetary value as it can be exchanged by the bearer for goods and services, thereby stimulating aggregate demand.

Some people believe that governments should print more money to solve the current financial crisis. However, only a small percentage of the money supply (3.5% in Australia) consists of physical notes and coins. The "real" money supply can be expanded in a number of ways including electronically with a few mouse clicks as the Rudd Government did with its $10.4 billion stimulus package. On top of this, the Reserve Bank of Australia has injected massive amounts of money (liquidity) into the financial system.

When central banks create (rather than print) money, this is referred to as credit money. Every time a financial institution makes a loan, new credit (money) is created. While it's true that consumers are presently reluctant to borrow and spend to help expand the money supply, the prevailing economic situation is not a money crisis, it's a credit crisis. Banks have been unwilling to lend to each other due to concerns that these loans may not be repaid.

Which is why governments and central banks are supplementing the borrowing and spending efforts of millions of people and propping up a range of business sectors, including banks. The US leads the bailout package stakes and has now spent more in financial assistance than it cost Uncle Sam to fund its involvement in World War II.

You'd have to cut down a forest of trees to print the currency necessary to pay for the greatest outlay of money in US history! Or you could print $200 million notes like Zimbabwe which now suffers hyperinflation as the massive and rapid increase in the amount of her currency has not been supported by growth in the output of goods and services. (Note: Zimbabwe recently released a $10 billion note).

Noted English economist, Tim Harford, believes the board game, Monopoly, is the perfect symbol of the financial crisis. Pity we can't print our way out of this mess with play money!

Posting Date: 27 January 2009

worldfacts

Recently, an interesting book landed on my desk. It was sent to me by *The Economist* as a reward for being a subscriber to their weekly print magazine. The book, *Pocket World in Figures*, is the 2015 edition of this annual tome produced by *The Economist*.

The book provides an intriguing snapshot of the world today on a diverse range of subjects. It gives rankings on everything from boozing to banking and commodities to computers. It even contains The Big Mac Index which is a light-hearted guide to whether currencies are at their "correct" level.

The digest contains a treasure trove of fascinating demographic data. Men in Sierra Leone can expect to live to just 45.1 years old. Women in Kuwait top the scales with regard to the percentage who are obese. Babies in New Caledonia have the highest infant mortality. And couples in Guam divorce more than those in any other nation.

Looking at the world through an economic lens is equally interesting. The US boasts the world's biggest economy. Monaco has the highest GDP per head of population. South Sudan has the lowest economic growth. The Euro zone is the biggest exporter. And Germany has the largest balance of payments surplus.

When it comes to public finances, the chart which captured my attention was government debt as a percentage of GDP. I have reproduced the chart below.

1	Japan	227.2		16	Netherlands	86.9
2	Greece	186.9		17	Germany	86.1
3	Italy	145.7		18	Slovenia	70.3
4	Portugal	135.4		19	Israel	68.4
5	Ireland	132.3		20	Finland	66.7
6	Iceland	129.5		21	Poland	66.0
7	France	113.0		22	Slovakia	59.0
8	United Kingdom	107.0		23	Denmark	58.8
9	Euro area	106.4		24	Czech Republic	58.6
10	Belgium	104.5		25	Sweden	52.0
11	United States	104.1		26	Switzerland	42.3
12	Spain	99.6		27	New Zealand	41.8
13	Canada	97.0		28	South Korea	35.6
14	Hungary	88.8		29	Australia	34.4
15	Austria	87.3		30	Norway	34.2

Regular readers of this blog know my frustration at the almost hysterical reaction we have in Australia to government debt. As I have repeatedly stated, it's a sweeping generalisation to say that public debt is inherently bad. Many economists agree that the actual amount of national public debt is less important than the percentage of debt to GDP.

A quick look at the chart reveals that Australia is not heavily indebted. In fact, we have the third lowest debt to GDP of OECD countries after Luxemburg and Estonia. Yet public debt remains a divisive issue in Australian politics and economics.

With government bond yields at near record lows, now is the time for the federal government to be borrowing more. Currently, the 10 year bond rate is just 2.34% (lower than during the 1930s depression!). That's the interest we would pay for 10 years even if the bond yield goes up during that period.

According to the economics editor for *The Age*, Peter Martin, the time is ripe to get some visionary projects off the drawing board. In a recent article, Martin argued that the current bond rates are "the deal of the century" and that Australia should borrow an extra $100 billion, as that would be enough to:

...build the long-awaited Brisbane to Sydney to Melbourne high-speed rail line, or to build Labor's original national broadband network, or Sydney's $11 billion WestConnex road project plus Melbourne's $11 billion metro rail project plus Melbourne's $16 billion East West Link plus something big in each of the other states.

Okay, enough of my hobby horse! Let's cycle back to the pocket guide and close this week's post with a look at living standards. As I have often opined, we definitely do live in the "lucky country" and the statistics in the pocket guide confirm that assertion.

In terms of world rankings, Australia sits in the number one position when it comes to secondary school enrolments as a percentage of the relevant age group. We are in the number two spot on the Human Development Index. And we occupy the third rung of the ladder on the Economic Freedom Index.

The Land of Oz is a pretty good place to live!

Posting Date: 23 March 2015

financialtips

Call me a Luddite, but I still shop for books in person at bookstores. Yes, I know I could go online and buy over the Internet. But as I explained in a previous post, *A library without books,* I love the smell and feel of books. Moreover, one of the benefits of visiting a bookstore is that you are exposed to titles outside your normal reading genre.

I know from experience that walking the aisles of a bookstore invariably means I'll discover something new or different. This occurred a few years ago when I was passing the popular science section and the protruding spine of a book with the provocative title, *How to Build a Time Machine*, piqued my interest. After thumbing the pages, I tentatively decided to buy a copy.

Written by internationally acclaimed Australian physicist, Paul Davies, *How to Build a Time Machine* is a light-hearted, tongue-in-cheek look at whether it's truly possible to build a machine that could transport a human to a different time. In theory, it can be done as long as you can construct a spaceship that can travel very close to the speed of light.

Davies explains that in an obvious sense we are all time travellers. "Do nothing," he writes, "and you will be conveyed inexorably into the future at the stately pace of one second per second." But to leap forward dramatically in time to reach the future sooner "you need an effective time machine". According to Davies, we can travel forward but what about backwards?

Davies believes that "travel into the past takes on an air of absurdity" as it would create "time travel paradoxes". He cites the example of a time traveller who goes back in time and murders his mother. "If (the) mother dies before giving birth, then the time traveller would never have existed. But in that case he would not be able to carry out the murder."

Even though we can't change the past, we humans have a tendency to "live" in the past. All of us have done things we wish we could do over. We have experienced embarrassing moments and made mistakes. How many times do we ask ourselves "If only I'd ..." or "I should have ..."? Alas, all the "what ifs" in the world can't undo the choices we made yesterday.

George Washington wrote: "To rectify past blunders is impossible, but we might profit by the experience of them." In the same vein, I've often heard it said that there are no mistakes in life, only lessons. My own view is that everyone has the opportunity to start afresh every single day and this certainly applies to one's finances.

Bad financial decisions can ruin your life and hurt those around you. In our must-have, consumer-orientated world it's easy to get caught in a web of unnecessary borrowing. Taking out a second credit card, buying the latest electronic gadgets, upgrading to the newest model vehicle and going on unaffordable holidays are common traps that, in some cases, lead to bankruptcy.

There's no doubt that poor financial decisions can come back to haunt you. In hindsight, you might regret some of the choices you made. The trick is not to repeat imprudent practices. As prevention is better than cure, here are some simple dos and don'ts to effective money management.

- **DO maintain a household budget** to track your spending, pay down debts and cut out wasteful discretionary expenditure.

- **DO save for a rainy day** and put away at least three months' worth of living expenses in case of emergency.

- **DO take out appropriate insurances** to cover unforeseen events like loss of income or damage to property.

- **DON'T take on "bad" debt** to finance day-to-day lifestyle purchases or impulse buying on credit cards.

- **DON'T put all your eggs in one basket** but reduce risk by investing in a variety of assets.

- **DON'T invest in things you know nothing about** and be wary of get-rich-quick schemes which offer too-good-to-be-true returns.

Here's to a bright financial future.

Posting Date: 21 November 2011

governance faultlines

In the original Star Wars movie Luke Skywalker (good guy) is pitted against Darth Vader (bad guy) in a high-tech space battle. As Luke manoeuvres his small strike fighter into position to attack Vader's giant command station - the Death Star - he switches off his futuristic targeting computer. Relying solely on instinct, Luke fires his torpedo and annihilates the Death Star.

Star Wars was first developed by George Lucas in the early post-Vietnam War era and is a classic example of art imitating life. America believed she would win the war against the Viet Cong because of her vastly superior technology and this created a false sense of invincibility.

The might of American technology - jet fighters, advanced weapons, sophisticated communications - was not able to defeat the cunning of the smaller Viet Cong. The technologically inferior South Vietnamese communist forces used a far more effective weapon - guerrilla warfare.

Fast forward to today, and despite electronic intercepts and billion dollar spy satellites, the US can't find any trace of the cagey Osama bin Laden. When it comes to warfare, history teaches us that technology alone is not the key to success and the same holds true in business.

Despite using advanced computer technology to identify and mitigate risk, the risk management systems in many financial institutions failed to pick up the brewing Global Financial Crisis (GFC). Banks around the world believed they were invincible and didn't realise the enemy was within their organisations.

The real adversary in the GFC was not a hostile invader but a far greater internal threat - poor corporate governance. Banks relied too heavily on mechanical models which did not generate red flags. As I argued in a recent blog post, many organisations did not have the right moral tone and this fostered a cavalier attitude to risk management.

The GFC was not a natural disaster - it was created by greed and lax supervision. In hindsight, the relentless pursuit of revenue growth in a world of easy credit should have rung alarm bells. Also, the real possibility of a housing downturn should have been included in risk assessments.

What is needed now is new thinking, not new technology. We need to take a hard look at risk appetites and risk management practices. Unless financial institutions implement better risk management controls and processes, one day we'll all have front row seats watching another slow train wreck unfold.

Posting Date: 31 August 2009

03 Social Changes

■■ Chapter Overview

Social forces are changing our world and the lives of individuals. We are living longer, marrying later and having fewer children. This is because our values, beliefs and attitudes are constantly evolving and impacting the way we live, work and think. Nowadays, we think differently about many things including health, education, the role of women and environmental issues. Changing demographics and social patterns are the focus of this chapter with discussion on population growth, higher education, estate planning, civil unrest and elite performance.

population growth

Somewhere in the world, right now, someone is being born. Every day, Mother Earth welcomes an average of 356,000 babies, according to UNICEF estimates. That's 14,833 births globally per hour, 247 births per minute or four births every second.

Births are one of two key demographic events that impact population growth - the other is deaths. Every day, 151,600 people leave the planet. This equates to 6,316 deaths globally per hour, 105 deaths per minute or almost two deaths every second.

Based on the aforementioned rates of "hatches" and "despatches", the Earth has a natural population increase of 204,400 people per day. Put another way, for every person who dies today another two babies will be born. This has pushed the number of humans living on Earth past the seven billion mark.

Notwithstanding the fact that we have been experiencing a rapid expansion of total population numbers, we are also simultaneously witnessing a fast slowdown of population growth. While this does seem counter-intuitive, it reflects the paradoxical era of population growth in which we are living.

On the one hand, the global improvement in life expectancy - a determinant of population growth - is working to increase the world's population. On the other hand, population aging is more than offset by falling global average fertility rates - another determinant of population growth.

The future size of the world's population is largely determined by the number of children women bear. If the average number of births per woman remains more than two, world population continues to increase. If, however, women on average have less than two births, then the world's population will eventually decrease.

A fertility rate of 2.1 births per woman (under low mortality conditions) is considered to be the magic number where couples have only enough children to replace themselves. This replacement level of fertility causes a country's population to slow down and eventually stabilise.

Nearly half the world's population has birth rates lower than 2.1. This is why many - but certainly not all - demographers believe that global population will peak in the coming decades. No one, however, can say with certainty when this peak will occur and what the pinnacle global population number will be.

What we do know is that one of the consequences of a fall in population growth will be a decline in the developed world's workforce. Europe in particular needs more babies to avert, in the words of *The Guardian*, "a population disaster" that will "imperil economic growth across the continent".

In that same article, released in August 2015, *The Guardian* noted:

> Record numbers of economic migrants and asylum-seekers are seeking to enter the European Union this summer and are risking their lives in the attempt. The paradox is that as police and security forces battle to keep them at bay, a demographic crisis is unfolding across the continent. Europe desperately needs more young people to run its health services, populate its rural areas and look after its elderly because, increasingly, its societies are no longer self-sustaining.

In a blog post I published in 2013 - *Global population aging* - I foreshadowed that nations might one day start competing for immigrants to bolster their workforces and I stand by that prediction. In the same post, I highlighted the acute demographic challenges facing Japan due to its very low birth rates - 1.21 children per woman.

In an earlier 2010 post - *The population debate* - I highlighted the unintended consequences of China's one-child policy on its workforce and noted that China's population was getting too old, too fast. Late last year, China changed its draconian one-child policy and now allows couples to have two children.

China's decision to relax its family planning laws was largely based on economic reasons. Its low fertility rate - between 1.2 and 1.5 children per woman - was driving the country towards economic crisis.

Sub-replacement fertility has spread across the planet with 115 countries maintaining fertility rates south of 2.1. In the short-term, this has benefits - as families get smaller they tend to become richer. Having fewer dependents results in increased discretionary income. This, in turn, drives greater consumption which is good for the economy.

Over the longer term, however, falling human reproduction is thought to be bad for the economy. It ultimately leads to decreased labour supply, higher labour costs, greater social welfare expenses, decreased taxation revenue and lower consumer demand.

It's clear that families are shrinking, but whether this is a cause for concern or celebration is subject to debate. I'm in the camp that believes the global spread of low fertility will have significant political, economic and social consequences. Our grandchildren will feel the full effects (both positive and negative) of this demographic megatrend.

Posting Date: 22 February 2016

civilunrest

Next Monday, I will publish my final blog post for 2011 and it will follow an established seasonal format. In what has quickly become an end-of-year tradition, next week's post will be the latest instalment in my annual *Night Before Christmas* parody series. I wrote my first Christmas parody in 2008 and followed that up with further parodies in 2009 and 2010.

It's good to finish the year on a light note, particularly as the past twelve month period has been challenging on many fronts. Mother Nature wreaked havoc in the form of tsunamis, earthquakes and floods. Human nature was just as unsettled, driving a wave of civil unrest around the world which turned city streets into unruly places.

We witnessed protests in Greece, revolts in Spain, strikes in Portugal, riots in London, rebellions in North Africa and a revolution in Egypt. On top of this, the Occupy Wall Street movement spread rapidly across the world like wildfire. From Seattle to Sydney, demonstrators took to the streets to voice their anger at what they see as financial and social inequality.

History teaches us that when revolutions take place, they are often hijacked by militant and extremist elements. This is what happened with the leaderless Occupy Wall Street movement which offered no official set of demands. As far as I can work out, the movement is *against* corporate greed and *for* economic justice.

In a year in which uprisings have gone global, the $64 million question is "why"? While each demonstration stems from divergent causes, I believe one common thread is a lack of economic growth. Younger people, in particular, have rallied against austerity measures and used social media networks to effectively organise themselves against authorities.

In good times - when people have jobs and can get ahead - the populace will tolerate inept governments and corporate excesses. But when the masses are suffering economic misery - limited job opportunities, bleak prospects and welfare cuts - they need to hold someone accountable for their pain. Social tension and unrest is now palpable throughout the world.

It is difficult to say how long this global discontent will continue, but what is clear is that individual protests feed off each other. A successful protest in one area spreads confidence that similar mass action will work elsewhere - even across national borders. This ripple effect was evident in the riots that started in London and spread quickly to other British cities.

Another root cause of the social upheavals is globalisation. The globalisation of information enables "protest fever" to spread rapidly across continents. Using Twitter, Facebook, YouTube and other technology platforms, protest organisers can quickly mobilise "flash mobs" to engage in civil disobedience. The real-time nature of social media has revolutionised popular political dissent.

A further impact of globalisation is interdependence. We now live in an interconnected world where nation-states are sensitive and vulnerable to events in far-away places. No country is insulated from what is happening elsewhere. We saw this during the Global Financial Crisis (GFC) where problems in the US subprime mortgage market created a global ripple effect.

A similar domino effect occurred with the Greek Sovereign Debt Crisis, which has degenerated into a systemic crisis of the Eurozone. The Greek contagion has spread to Italy and other European nations may well fall victim. Deep divisions have emerged between the Eurozone's 17 member countries.

Germany's stance has fuelled anger among citizens in Greece and Spain who are unhappy with the austerity measures demanded by Berlin.

It's clear we are living through very challenging economic times and have entered a new era of civil unrest. The middle class has become revolutionary. Workers are outraged at the lack of economic opportunity. Citizens feel betrayed by their political representatives. World financial markets are alarmed and European unity is under threat.

With the European Union recently warning that the Eurozone could slip back into recession, 2012 is going to present further social and economic challenges. On-going austerity will likely fuel a fresh wave of mass rallies. In many parts of the world, peace and prosperity in the New Year will be elusive. It's a shame that the upcoming season of goodwill will be so short-lived.

Posting Date: 12 December 2011

gametheory

We humans are prone to panic when we sense danger - it's part of our genetic wiring. The body instinctively triggers a fight or flee response as a self-preservation mechanism and this gave early homo-sapiens the energy to battle assailants or escape predators.

In lieu of protecting you and/or enhancing your chances of survival, this primitive biological response to stress can actually cause unnecessary harm by driving "every-man-for-himself" behaviour. Such self-defeating conduct can be seen in all walks of life.

The mere threat of a fuel strike immediately causes panic buying with queues of angry motorists rushing to service stations to top up their tanks. Similarly, panic buying occurs when there are rumours of grocery shortages, driving shoppers to fill their trolleys and clear supermarket shelves.

Scampering to purchase petrol before rationing begins or hoarding groceries prior to stocks being depleted are, at an individual level, seemingly sensible things to do. Such behaviour, however, is based on the (flawed) logic that if you don't act promptly and everyone else does, you will be worse off.

This same self-interested and self-defeating rationale applies in a financial crisis. If depositors get whiff of a failure they move promptly to pull their money out of their financial institution. Depositors swoop in the belief that withdrawals will be paid on a first come, first served basis.

But under a fractional reserve banking system, no financial institution has sufficient cash on hand to concurrently repay every single depositor in full, on demand. Thus, a bank run is often a self-fulfilling process - the fear of a bank failure can actually cause a bank to fail.

In days gone by, bank runs were very public and dramatic events with queues of irate people snaked around branches demanding their money back. Today, visibly panicked mobs in the street have been largely replaced by invisible electronic withdrawals at the click of a mouse.

It has been observed that bank solvency is a social phenomenon because what customers believe about a financial institution can determine its fate. When people see other savers emptying their accounts, they too rush to do the same. Yet, all depositors would be better off if a run did not happen in the first place.

It's clear that the mere threat of vacant shelves, empty bowsers or cashless banks exacerbates panic. So, how do you stop motorists, shoppers and savers panicking in the first place? Maybe a sign which says "walk, don't run" might help? Or perhaps a warning to "look before you leap"?

The harsh reality is that we have to get better as a society in responding to the surprises and shocks of modern living. This requires us to take a more holistic approach by focussing on "we" rather than "me". Our narrow self-interests must give way to the optimum outcome for all parties.

Trying to achieve the best for the collective rather than the individual led to the development of game theory. I explained game theory in an earlier post, *How to make the world a better place*. Game theory examines how individuals react given the actions of someone else.

According to game theory, an individual tries to predict what his/her opponents will do and then chooses strategies that will provide him/her with the best payoff. Put crudely, it's about the way we manipulate situations for our own personal advantage.

But as we have just seen, acting in one's self-interest does not always serve one's self-interest. Paradoxically, if each individual stayed calm in a crisis, the outcome would be better for everyone. I live in hope that one day we may see individuals cooperating for the common good, even if it means personal loss.

Posting Date: 21 October 2013

education imperative

Education is one of the most important investments an individual can make. It is also critical for the long-term prosperity of a nation. Levels of education and training are directly related to workforce productivity. The key to a skilled workforce is a high-quality education system. Our prosperity as a nation, therefore, rests on having schools that can compete with the best in the world.

The Federal Government's recently released review of education funding - the Gonski report - underscores that Australia's economy, its future and its prosperity are intrinsically tied to educating our young people. The report goes to the heart of the productivity debate with the Business Council of Australia noting that "a high-performing education system is fundamental to Australia's competitiveness and supporting long-term productivity growth".

Gonski wants an extra $5 billion a year for school education to reverse the decline in Australia's school performance. In the past 10 years, Australian children have slipped from being equal second in reading among OECD countries to being equal seventh. They have also fallen from equal fifth to equal thirteenth in maths. The report warns that Australian students are falling behind their counterparts in Asia.

Prime Minister Gillard said it was impossible to achieve "the economy we will need tomorrow if we lose the education race today". However, she refused to commit to specific budgetary measures to improve education outcomes. The government remains cautious about any spending which could derail its chances of a 2012-13 budget surplus.

The report argues that parents' capacity to contribute financially should be taken into account when determining the level of government support to non-government schools. It is estimated that one-third of Australian parents will still pay school fees. The government cannot guarantee that private school fees won't rise as a result of the new funding model proposed by Gonski.

Figures from the Australian Scholarships Group show the cost of putting a child through 13 years of private schooling could reach almost $500,000. Parents who choose government schooling for a child born in 2011 can expect to pay over $75,000 for their education. Notwithstanding whether the 41 recommendations in the Gonski report are eventually taken up in whole or part by the Government, education will remain costly for Australian families.

Despite the cost, an increasing number of families are committed to helping their children get a better and higher education. Today, education beyond high school is practically a necessity to build a better life. Tertiary education invariably leads to a higher paying career, more secure employment and a greater choice of jobs.

While a tertiary qualification is regarded as the pathway to success, it comes at a significant price. Australia has the third highest university fees out of all OECD countries, after the United States and Japan. Not surprisingly, one-third of Australian university students live with their parents and finish university with a HECS debt. However, this initial financial burden is more than made up by the financial gains that follow over a lifetime.

Australia's ambition to become the "clever country" will not become a reality unless we spend more on education. Given the Federal Government's strident mantra of education as one of its highest priorities, it should move expeditiously to inject the extra funding, identified by Gonski, into the education system.

Posting Date: 12 March 2012

graduate glut

Too many university graduates and not enough jobs - this is the situation in many countries around the world. There is growing unease that nations are producing an oversupply of educated workers. This is forcing graduates to do jobs that do not require their qualification.

Last year in Australia, 65% of high school students (Year 12) applied for university. Those that complete their degree will add to the proportion of Australians with tertiary qualifications. This figure jumped to 25% in 2012, up from only 3% of adults with university degrees in 1970.

Australians are more highly educated than ever before and the number with degrees is rising. The federal government has set an ambitious target for 40% of young Australians (25-34 years) to have a bachelor's degree or better by 2025.

The opening of university admission floodgates has seen undergraduate student numbers soar. Meanwhile, the number of school leavers undertaking apprenticeships in the trades is falling. According to University of Canberra vice-chancellor, Stephen Parker, Australia risks becoming a country full of university graduates who can't get a plumber when they need one.

There are increasing calls for state governments around Australia to overhaul secondary school curriculum. A recent report claims that schools in NSW are not equipping young people with the skills they need for the workplace. The prevailing school culture favours traditional academic subjects with an emphasis on entry to university.

A counter view regarding graduate numbers can be found in a discussion paper on Australia's future workforce needs. In that paper, the Australian Workforce and Productivity Agency states:

...we see that the demand for higher levels of skill is a reality. Our scenarios and modelling confirm that this can be expected to continue into the future in response to technology-induced change, structural adjustment, a progressive shift to services-based industries, and Australia's changing demographics. Increasing globalisation is another factor affecting the demand for higher-level skills, with Asia a burgeoning market for Australian services.

The report goes on to quote the OECD:

In order to prosper in today's economy, local communities increasingly need to ensure that they adequately invest in education and skills. Higher-level skills, such as the ability to analyse and process complex information, be creative and communicate effectively, are all increasing in importance in the context of the knowledge-based economy ... It is more and more likely that future jobs will demand higher skills levels, as low-skilled jobs are lost and redefined in the current restructuring process.

It's clear that planning for Australia's future workforce needs is not an easy task. We all know that human capital is the key to our success as a nation and that we need a skilled and diverse workforce. But what should the composition of that workforce be?

Right now in Australia, there is an undersupply of workers in some trades (e.g., bricklaying). At the same time, there is an oversupply of workers in some professions (e.g., teaching). Clearly, the system is not perfect and we need to examine how to better balance the workforce skills mix.

Industry demand for skilled workers is not keeping up with the rapid supply in higher education. Enrolment targets could be set which would enable the labour market to absorb graduates. However, this would take us back to the now discarded system of imposing limits on university places.

Our rising level of imports from low wage countries is reducing the demand for low skilled workers. Simultaneously, technology is increasing the demand for higher skilled workers. In lieu of focussing on short-term fixes, our decision making needs to be informed by the longer-term and the undeniable trend to more skilled workers.

The harsh reality is that in Australia - and around the world - labour market groups with higher skill levels typically enjoy lower unemployment rates. The corollary of this is that many welfare recipients are unskilled as demand for their services has fallen.

I remain of the view, as I espoused in an earlier post, *Education imperative*, that education is one of the most important investments an individual can make. Today, education beyond high school is practically a necessity to build a better life in the "knowledge economy".

Posting Date: 13 April 2015

great oratory

Friends, Romans, countrymen and readers of this blog, lend me your ears. I come to lament the passing of great oratory. Throughout the ages, persuasive speeches hath motivated and inspired people to fight injustice, confront disasters and lay down their life for a worthy cause. But words alone can't solve a financial crisis, as the Ancient Romans discovered. The great Roman orator, Cicero, gave his people the following advice:

> The budget should be balanced, the treasury should be refilled, public debt should be reduced, the arrogance of officialdom should be tempered and controlled, and the assistance to foreign lands should be curtailed, lest Rome become bankrupt. People must again learn to work, instead of living on public assistance.

Hmm…smart guy! Problem is the Romans didn't listen to Cicero. Ironically, the Roman Empire eventually collapsed due to out-of-control government spending and over regulation of the economy - it abandoned free market capitalism and became a socialist state. Even though Cicero's pleas fell on deaf ears, words can and have changed the course of history when masterly constructed and eloquently delivered.

In my home bookcase sits a wonderful book called *Lend Me Your Ears: Great Speeches In History*. It's a weighty tome of over 1,000 pages and includes more than 200 examples of outstanding oratory by men and women from past to present. Covering addresses by figures from Greek philosopher, Socrates, to US president, George Bush, *Lend Me Your Ears* demonstrates the power of words to lift hearts, provide hope and engage audiences.

The book contains an instructive preface on the art of speechmaking. The book's editor, himself a past White

House speechwriter, reveals the vital elements of a great speech. One of those elements is a technique called anaphora. Anaphora is a figure of speech that describes the repetition of a word or phrase at the beginning of successive sentences, clauses or phrases.

Arguably, the most famous anaphora is Martin Luther King's phrase, "*I have a dream*," in which each repetition of that clause introduced a fresh elaboration of his message. Churchill's famous defiance of Hitler, "…*we shall fight* on the beaches, *we shall fight* on the landing grounds, *we shall fight* in the fields…" is another striking example of anaphora.

Another popular rhetorical device is epiphora. In direct contrast to anaphora, epiphora is the repetition of a word or phrase at the end of a sentence. Ending sentences with the same word order was used very successfully by Barack Obama during his 2008 campaign for president. The slogan *"Yes we can"* completed numerous paragraphs in speeches and became globally recognised as a powerful rallying cry.

To embed key messages, President Obama uses a further rhetorical technique called - in literary parlance - tricolon. A tricolon is a series of three words, phrases or sentences that are parallel in structure and rhythm. I began this post by paraphrasing Shakespeare's classic tricolon - *"Friends Romans and countrymen"*. Examples of this rule of three in linguistics can be found everywhere in Western culture.

Abraham Lincoln used the tricolon, *"Government of the people, by the people, for the people"* during the Gettysburg Address. The Olympic Motto, *"Faster, Higher, Stronger"* utilises a tricolon framework as do phrases such as *"The Good, the Bad, and the Ugly"*. Even Steve Jobs got in on the act and told us that the iPad 2 was *"thinner, lighter and faster"*.

Obama has been referred to as The New Cicero and is well

known for his use of tricolon. An example can be found in the president's speech at the funeral of Nelson Mandela wherein he said: *"And when the night grows dark, when injustice weighs heavy on our hearts, when our best-laid plans seem beyond our reach, let us think of Madiba…"*

It can be seen that great oration is much more than just standing in front of a podium and murmuring a few words. It takes planning and preparation and the right use of rhetorical techniques to stir emotions. With training and perseverance, you too can learn to make jaw-dropping presentations that will electrify your audience and win their hearts and minds.

Posting Date: 20 July 2015

misleading averages

Many years ago I attended a business conference where the keynote speaker sounded a note of caution about the word "average". To illustrate his point, he told a joke about a man with one foot in a bucket of boiling water and the other foot in a bucket of freezing water. The man subjected to the excruciating extremes of temperature exclaimed that "on average" he felt comfortable.

For humour to be effective there has to be some truth present, which is why the joke's punch-line drew laughter from the audience. The underlying message from the keynote speaker was clear: Averages can be very misleading. This is particularly the case where outliers can completely throw off an entire data set, rendering the average figure entirely meaningless.

For example, imagine there are 50 people in a room and each has assets totalling $500,000. This means the average assets per person is $500,000. Now imagine that one person leaves the room and is replaced by the world's richest man - Bill Gates.

The inclusion of the Microsoft founder in the sample group causes the average assets per person to skyrocket to over a billion dollars - which is grossly misleading as only one is actually a billionaire. Yet the "average" wealth result gives the impression that all the people in the group are much better off than they really are.

It takes just one unrepresentative outlier to pull the average in their direction. This is why it's said that averages conceal rather than reveal. Averages can obscure vital differences and mask important similarities. Just knowing the average of something does not tell the whole story.

Let's take customer satisfaction surveys. One satisfied

customer plus one dissatisfied customer does not make a "neutral" customer. You can't average people and their attitudes but this has not stopped the misuse and misinterpretation of customer survey data.

As crazy as it sounds most people - statistically speaking - have more than the average number of legs. While the overwhelming majority of humans have two legs, some have one leg while others have none due to birth defects and/or accidents. When you mathematically calculate the average of every person on the planet, the resultant number is pulled down by those with less than two legs.

Allow me to provide a more pragmatic example of the flaw with averages. Take a household consisting of three generations of the one family - from young children to grandparents. If you add together the ages of the family members and divide by the number of members, this produces an average age that has absolutely no meaning whatsoever.

Another example which is closer to home for me is credit card debt in Australia. Statistically, the average credit card debt per household is $5,600. There are nine million households in Australia and 6.57 million of them have absolutely no credit card debt.

This makes the average credit card debt figure for all households meaningless. A more accurate measure would be to calculate the average credit card debt for the 2.43 million households with a credit card. This figure is much higher (and more realistic) at $20,800.

Notwithstanding their shortcomings, people love averages. We humans are keen to know where we stand when measured against the average - average height, average weight, average income, average intelligence and so on. In doing so, we typically ignore just how wrong the picture is that averages paint of the world.

To be fair, in some instances the use of averages is perfectly valid and revealing. But this is only the case if what you're trying to average is uniform and not skewed in any way. Beyond that, statistical averages have caused many a wise man to opine on their unreliability.

> Then there is the man who drowned crossing a stream with an average depth of six inches. *W.I.E. Gates*

> Facts are stubborn things, but statistics are pliable. *Mark Twain*

> There are three types of lies - lies, damn lies and statistics. *Benjamin Disraeli*

Let me end with my own statement of the blindingly obvious: Our knowledge of averages is below average.

Posting Date: 29 February 2016

estate planning

There's no escaping the fact that one day we are all going to die. While I don't wake up every morning thinking about my inevitable demise, I do have plans in place to ensure my wishes are carried out when I am no longer here. The Australian Securities and Investments Commission estimates that nearly half of all Australians have not prepared a last Will and Testament.

Younger people, in particular, believe that preparing a Will is only for "oldies". They are too busy living life to the full to be worried about some distant morbid event. But eventually we will all be confronted by our mortality and death often catches us by surprise. Such was the case with Sam - a fictitious character based on a real-life scenario.

Sam was always going to get around to preparing a Will. Unfortunately, he didn't. He died unexpectedly and if the shock of his death wasn't enough for his de-facto wife, Cheryl, and their son, the bigger shock came when Sam's former wife made a claim on the estate on behalf of the children of his first marriage.

As Sam died without a Will, he is said to have died intestate. If you die intestate, your estate is administered according to the relevant state's *Succession Act* covering "intestate succession". Even though Cheryl was aware of what Sam wanted to do with his money, the legislation did not give effect to his intentions.

Cheryl knew that as a de-facto partner she had inheritance rights under the *Succession Act* but discovered that a spouse doesn't automatically "get it all" if children are involved. As Sam did not have a Will identifying those who were to inherit and what each would inherit, certain of his relatives became beneficiaries in the proportions set out by the Act.

To make matters worse, there was an argument over the funeral arrangements and another over whether Sam did or did not want to donate his organs. Also, a dispute arose over a charitable gift to one of Sam's favourite aid agencies. Further complications arose over Sam's self-managed super fund and the payment of death benefits.

These conflicts could have been avoided if Sam had a Will specifying his funeral wishes and the bequests he wanted to make. He could also have appointed an enduring guardian to make medical decisions on his behalf and instructed that person that his usable organs were to be donated following his death.

It can be seen that dying without a Will is rife with problems. An intestate death invariably causes unnecessary hardship and extra work for family and dependants. It also means the government may become the default administrator of your affairs. This is why you should safeguard the interests of your family, friends and dependants and make a Will.

Death is a morose subject and most people don't want to talk about it let alone plan for it. But like taxes, death is inevitable and that's why estate planning is a must for everyone. More than just a Will, an estate plan takes into account your superannuation, powers of attorney and the appointment of an enduring guardian.

Contrary to popular opinion, Wills and estate planning are not the exclusive domain of the rich. Making a Will is the best way to make sure your estate is passed on to family and friends exactly as you wish. So, don't leave your estate to chance. If you don't have a Will, you're making a deadly mistake.

Posting Date: 6 July 2015

writer's block

What do you do when you're responsible for publishing a weekly blog and suddenly discover you have run out of ideas? Week in and week out you pound the keyboard producing what you hope is elegant prose. Then one week you have "brain fog" and a blank screen is frustratingly staring back at you.

You know not to panic as even the best writers face a time of dryness when the words stop flowing. You also know it's not caused by a sudden drop in energy or lack of motivation but the absence of an interesting topic. All of the things you want to write about have been covered in previous posts you have published.

But you can't throw in the towel as the requirement to crank out another post drives your need to find new content. Seeking inspiration from others, you trawl (unsuccessfully) through the daily business news looking for a theme around which you can impart something of interest to your readers. Then, without notice, it hits you like a ton of bricks - write a blog post about writer's block.

There are occasions when all of us can be lost for words when putting pen to paper or fingers on the keyboard. Without doubt, the most difficult part of writing for many people is actually getting started. Novelist, Ernest Hemingway, said the most frightening thing he ever encountered was "a blank sheet of paper". I think a modern analogy would be the tormenting blink of a cursor.

Clearly, an empty page or a blank screen can be intimidating, so the trick is to get some words down quickly. Don't spend too much time searching for the right words or clever turn of phrases to satisfy your inner critic. It is rare that something can be written perfectly the first time. A rough draft can always be polished and improved later.

A technique some writers use - and one I utilised during my business studies - is to start writing at whatever point you like. MBA essays typically begin with an executive summary which most students understandably write AFTER completing their essays. I, however, wrote my summary BEFORE I even started my essay as it gave me an outline and overall sense of direction.

I then wrote the introduction and, believe it or not, a draft conclusion before starting the body of the essay. This essay writing methodology, which any student can use, is not as bizarre as it sounds. It provides a roadmap which stops you veering off in the wrong direction and informs you in advance of your ultimate destination so that you can organise your thoughts accordingly.

While orderly progression in your writing is not essential, having a plan of attack is highly desirable. So, don't wing it and don't confuse writer's block with procrastination. Also, avoid the mistake of thinking you have to complete one writing project from go to woe before starting another.

I spend most of my professional life writing and communicating and become bored easily if I work exclusively on just one task. I work on multiple writing projects at a time (e.g., board reports, staff updates, member correspondence, PowerPoint presentations, blog posts, etc.) switching back and forth from one writing project to another. This variety keeps my creative juices flowing.

Probably the best advice I've come across about crashing through writer's block is to just start writing. That's exactly what I did to produce this post - I wrote about the fact that I didn't know what to write about and the end result is another blog post. In the process, I moved emotionally from initially having a sinking feeling to ultimately feeling a sigh of relief.

At the end of the day, there is no catchall solution to driving output when it's time to write. But when your creative well is dry and you are feeling uninspired, you just can't give up. Hopefully, the tips and techniques I have shared here will help you get the words out of your head and onto the page - and that's gotta be a good start. Happy writing!

Posting Date: 13 May 2013

timepoverty

Trust me, I get it. Life is busy. We are working longer hours and are under constant pressure. We try to fit more and more into every day. Many of us function in a state of near exhaustion. Despite having every labour saving device imaginable, we remain time poor.

The 21st century is very demanding. We are on call 24/7 thanks to "anywhere, anytime" computing. Surrounded by technology in our homes and workplaces, we have constant information at our fingertips delivered by smartphones and other mobile devices.

The rhythm of our lives is in high gear, yet we crave a less frenetic existence. Technology was meant to be a blessing but it has become a curse. Washing machines, microwaves and the Internet have not given us more time. Busyness has become a way of life.

Living in an iWorld means staying plugged in. Technology has become a drug which is hard to turn off. For many, checking emails before breakfast and after dinner is the norm. The electronic transformation of work has intruded into our private lives.

Time is money and it seems we don't want to waste a second of this precious resource. Unlike other resources, time cannot be accumulated - we all use up 24 hours each day. The more demands that are made on our time, the less downtime we have.

So how do we get time back? Time, like all commodities, is subject to the laws of supply and demand. We are each supplied with the exact same amount and it's not possible to buy an additional supply of hours. Our focus, therefore, should be on controlling our time, but this is easier said than done.

Leisure time, once plentiful, is now scarce and elusive. With expanding workweeks, opportunities for rest and relaxation are diminishing. Paradoxically, we are so busy seeking the good life, we have little time to enjoy the fruits of our labour even if we can afford it.

Our calendars are crammed, but it wasn't meant to be this way. Futurists long ago told us that 21st century technological wizardry would reduce the need for labour. Automation was supposed to usher in a fifteen hour working week causing all of us to be bored with an over-abundance of leisure time.

For some, being busy has become a status symbol. It makes us feel important and valued. It satisfies our need to be needed. We crave the adrenalin rush of being a super-achiever. We thrive on the adulation of being a doer and a go-to person for problem solving.

"Time famine" is an epidemic afflicting all developed nations. Growing affluence comes at a cost. It seems that the more we have, the more we want. Rampant consumerism has caused us to confuse a good life with a goods life. We want the latest and best possessions, putting us on a hedonic treadmill.

In Australia, we definitely suffer the curse of the rat race. Contrary to our popular image, we are not a nation of laidback beach dwellers. Our work-life balance is out of kilter. Increasingly, we live to work and not work to live. Households - particularly those with young families - are strapped for time.

It is clear that the world has become stuck in fast-forward. According to Carl Honoré, author of *In Praise of Slow: How a Worldwide Movement is Challenging the Cult of Speed,* we need to slow down and rebel against a hectic lifestyle.

In an earlier post, I reviewed *In Praise of Slow*. It's a useful "how to" guide for anyone who is tired of constantly living in the fast lane. Of course, you'll have to make time in your busy schedule to go out and buy a copy and then you'll have to find time to read it. But it will be a productive investment of time.

You never know, it may even change how you work, rest and play!

Posting Date: 7 March 2016

elite performance

During my recent trip to London, I had one of those serendipitous moments. To kill some time while waiting for my wife to finish at the hairdresser, I popped into a nearby bookstore. While browsing, I unexpectedly discovered a book on a topic I had been thinking about only a week earlier - peak performance in sport and the lessons this offers for excelling in any field of endeavour.

On flicking through the book, I was immediately drawn to the author's central premise: Success is possible for all of us, but requires hard work and self-belief rather than innate ability. While this may sound simplistic and old fashioned, it certainly resonates with me, which is why I found Matthew Syed's book, *Bounce: The myth of talent and the power of practice*, an interesting read.

Syed is a former international table tennis champion turned sports writer. His book is replete with powerful lessons about what drives elite performance. He draws on ground-breaking work in psychology and neuroscience to uncover the secrets of top athletes. The recurring theme of his book is that talent is not genetically determined nor is excellence preordained. Rather, success on the sporting field (and in any other area of life) is based on "purposeful practice".

According to Syed, there are no shortcuts to success. Rather, it takes 10,000 hours of purposeful practice to make a sporting champion. This is intensive practice with clear and challenging aims. Most of us practice things that we can already do. However, the most effective practice is when you repeatedly try something new which is beyond your current capability until you master it.

The 10,000 hours of focussed and deliberate practice is based on studies by Swedish psychologist, Dr. K. Anders Ericsson, the results of which were published in *Psychological*

Review in 1993. Ericsson's theory was popularised by Malcolm Gladwell in his book, *Outliers: The Story of Success*. As Syed outlines in *Bounce*, many great sportspeople (and high achievers in other fields) reached their 10,000 hours of practice early in life.

Examples include Tiger Woods, Venus Williams and even Mozart. These individuals were not child prodigies who were naturally blessed with amazing skills. Rather, they were all beneficiaries of extraordinary upbringings. Each had parents who introduced them to a particular activity at a very early age and lavished them with parental training, support and encouragement behind the scenes. Each child practised unusually hard over many years to excel.

Tiger Woods is a good example of someone who epitomises the rigours of practice. His father understood the importance of early practice and gave Tiger a golf club shortly before his first birthday. Initially Tiger practised at home and at eighteen months had his first golf outing. By the age of three, Tiger's practice sessions took place on the driving range and putting green where he would hone his skills for hours at a time. "By his mid-teens," Syed notes, "Woods had clocked ten thousand hours of dedicated practice, just like Mozart."

While extolling the benefits of purposeful practice in sport and the arts, Syed laments that it is not practised in business. Talent management in organisations is void of the expert mentoring and coaching that one sees on the sporting field. "Tasks," according to Syed, "are often repetitive and boring and fail to push employees to their creative limits and beyond" with objective feedback "...often comprising little more than a half-hearted annual review".

The prevailing view in many organisations is that supervisors do not need specific skills in the functions they oversee, just general knowledge and talent as a manager. Syed challenges this conventional wisdom using the example of a UK government minister who changed portfolios seven times in seven years. "This is no less absurd than rotating Tiger Woods from golf to football to ice hockey to baseball and expecting him to perform expertly in every arena," argues Syed.

To further prosecute his case, Syed cites the collapse of Enron as an example of poor talent management. Enron believed in the philosophy espoused by management consultants, McKinsey & Company, that "talent is what ultimately determines success and failure in the corporate world; that pure reasoning ability matters far more than domain-specific knowledge". Enron learned the hard way that having industry specific knowledge and experience is also important.

Please allow me to end this post by pointing out that the much-vaunted 10,000-hour rule has many critics. It has been variously called a bogus threshold, an over-simplification and even a myth. The critics may well be right in saying that 10,000 is not a magical figure. Regardless, we all know that it takes copious practice to be the world's best at any task. Greatness requires enormous time - however long that may be.

Posting Date: 19 October 2015

creditunions

Since 1948, credit unions around the world have set aside the third Thursday in October to celebrate International Credit Union Day. This international day of observance brings people together to reflect upon their cooperative history, their credit union achievements and to promote the credit union idea across the world.

The theme for International Credit Union Day 2015 is *"People Helping People"*. With over 57,000 credit unions in 103 countries, International Credit Union Day is an open invitation to more than 208 million members to share the credit union experience. Celebrations in different countries take place in many forms.

The worldwide credit union movement traces its origins back to nineteenth century Germany and a man named Friedrich Wilhelm Raiffeisen. During a famine in 1846/47 Raiffeisen, the mayor of a rural village, was appalled by the activities of moneylenders and their treatment of peasant farmers. The farmers were facing financial ruin as a result of a severe drought.

The exorbitant financing rates required by opportunistic lenders prevented the farmers from borrowing money to help them survive the crisis. In response, a group of landowners under the guidance of Mayor Raiffeisen banded together, pooling their money to provide low-cost loans to their fellow farmers in need. The interest on the loans provided a dividend for the savers' investment. Thus, the first credit cooperative was born.

After a slow start, other Raiffeisen credit societies or "village banks" began to spring up all over Germany. The concept of *people helping people* found universal appeal and credit unions took roots in other lands. The first American credit union was established by Alphonse Desjardins, a Canadian journalist, who in 1900 founded a caisse populaire (people's cooperative bank) in Quebec.

In 1909, Desjardins formed the first credit union in the USA. This attracted the attention of American businessman, Edward Filene, who was first introduced to financial cooperatives in India in 1907. A wealthy retailer, Filene was also an innovative man who looked for long-term solutions to widespread problems. He became convinced of the value of credit unions and personally donated more than $1m to help organise credit unions throughout the US.

In 1920 Filene hired a charismatic lawyer, Roy Bergengren, to be the managing director of the Massachusetts Credit Union Association and he worked tirelessly to open new credit unions. It wasn't until after the Second World War that the credit union movement reached Australia. Kevin Yates had observed credit unions during his military service in Canada and this inspired him to pioneer a similar set of social reform principles in Australia.

In 1946, Yates established the Catholic Thrift and Loan Co-operative Limited in Sydney, which later became known as Universal Credit Union. *"Not for profit, not for charity but for service"* was the slogan as credit unions began to appear across all states of Australia. Like their credit union counterparts in other parts of the world, Australia's early credit unions were organised around a "common bond".

This bond between members was usually occupational, social or determined by neighbourhood. Within the bond, membership was open to all regardless of race, religion, economic or social status. Each member had one vote regardless of the amount of his/her savings. The members, who elected a board of directors, held control of the credit union.

Working people, to defeat usury, formed Australian credit

unions. These "backyard bankers" enjoyed phenomenal growth in the sixties. In the seventies they became one of Australia's biggest providers of personal loans. And in the eighties Australian credit unions collectively pioneered many innovations in financial services including the first to operate ATMs in Australia and the first to pay interest monthly on term deposits.

Today over four million Australians are members of one of the nation's 92 member owned financial institutions. Australia's credit unions form an important part of this sector which has assets of more than $94bn. The sector also manages the fifth largest holding of deposits for Australian households with balances close to $80bn.

The credit union movement began 160 years ago with a simple but radical idea - that with the help of your neighbours, you can improve your financial well-being. Even after all this time, the bedrock principles of credit unions remain unchanged. Credit unions are still about people coming together to be their own bank by pooling their savings to provide each other affordable credit. In short, *people helping people*.

I hope you enjoyed this brief credit union history. Have a great International Credit Union Day this Thursday. And remember, anyone can join a credit union and everyone should.

Posting Date: 12 October 2015

boldambitions

Shortly after I started my banking career over three decades ago with one of the major banks, a senior bank executive said something I've never forgotten. He told a group of new recruits that people can be divided into two categories - players and spectators.

He explained that spectators never enter the field of play. Rather, they sit in the safety and anonymity of the grandstand where they boo and hiss. They yell gratuitous instructions to the players and pass judgment but never actually pull on a jersey themselves and have a go.

The players, on the other hand, are the people who roll up their sleeves and give it their all. They don't always cross the line and score when they get the ball. However, they do experience the joy of participating and striving to overcome the odds to become a winner.

In the game of life, a player takes action to achieve a desired outcome. A spectator, in contrast, is at the mercy of choices others make. I've always been a player and not a bench warmer. I know that life is not a spectator sport. I want to have a stake in life and not watch it go by.

Yet the world is full of people who will tell you why you can't do something. We were told we should not build the Sydney Opera House. The naysayers were also against the cost of our national Parliament House in Canberra. And don't forget the critics who were opposed to Sydney hosting the 2000 Olympics.

Aren't you glad we didn't listen? We would have missed out on two national icons and the best Olympic Games ever. Just as individuals need to have a go, so do nations. I'm proud to be an Aussie and know that this nation can punch above its weight.

Why doesn't Sydney set itself the goal of becoming the financial capital of Asia? Surely we are as good as Singapore, Shanghai or Seoul? A number of Asian cities are working hard to raise their profile and give Hong Kong a run for its money. We too should be in that race - let's have a go!

While we're at it, why don't we overhaul our tax system to make us more competitive in a globalised world? That was one of the drivers behind the Henry Review of our taxation system. But the government has largely ignored the committee's 138 recommendations. All is not lost - we can still have a go at reforming our tax system to position Australia to deal with the challenges of the 21st century.

And let's not forget the need to change education funding. That need was identified in the Gonski Report which the government has also not actioned. Educating our young people is critical to Australia's economy and its long-term prosperity. We need schools that can compete with the best in the world. Let's have a go at keeping up with the finest education systems.

In our personal lives, our deeds need to be as bold as our ambitions and so it is in public life. Half measures never get us to where we want to go. Our political leaders can't be big on rhetoric and slow on action. Rather, they must embrace opportunities to secure our nation's future. Let's not be afraid to have a go.

Posting Date: 18 June 2012

latin lesson

The English language is replete with words of Latin origin. Around 80% of the entries in any English dictionary are borrowed, mainly from Latin. Given this etymology, Latin is alive and well in many of the words and phrases we use today.

You might be surprised at how much Latin you know - without actually knowing it. Words like *exit, circa, alumni, impromptu, ante, bonus, emeritus, scholar, facsimile, naive, sacrosanct, ubiquity, academia, halo, hiatus, papacy* and *tempest* are all derived from Latin.

We are also very comfortable in using Latin abbreviations such as etc. (which stands for *et cetera and translates as* "and the rest"), i.e. (*id est or* "that is"), e.g. (*exempli gratia or* "for example"), N.B. (*nota bene or* "note well"), et al. (*et alii or* "and other people") and viz (*videlicet or* "namely").

When it comes to Latin phrases we are equally at ease. Some popular phrases which roll off the tongue include *ad nauseam* ("to the point of sickness"), *caveat emptor* ("let the buyer beware"), *quid pro quo* ("something for something") and *persona non grata* ("an unwelcome person").

The legal profession loves to throw around Latin words from Ancient Rome's legal system. Common legal terms used today include *alibi* ("at another place"), *alias* ("at another time called"), *affidavit* ("he pledged") and *subpoena* ("under penalty").

While progress has been made in translating legal writing into plain English, old Latin phrases still appear in legal contracts. It is not unusual to see terms like *fiduciary* ("held in trust"), *ex gratia* ("out of kindness"), *verbatim* ("word for word") and *ceteris paribus* ("all other things being equal").

Bankers have also borrowed (pun intended) from Latin. The influence of Latin can be seen in financial terms like debit (from *debere* - "to owe"), credit (from *credere* - "to entrust"), percent (from *per centum* - "by the hundred") and endorse (from *in dorsum* - "on the back").

The second oldest profession in the world, politics (*politicus* - "citizen of the state") is replete with Latin words. The English derivative of the Latin word *senex* ("old man") is the word senate (referring to a council of elders). To make a law, a parliament (*parliamentum*) enacts legislation. The term, legislation, is derived from two Latin words - *legis* ("law") and *latum* ("to make").

The influence of Latin is also evident in the naming of countries. The Latin name *Britannia* survived the Roman withdrawal from Britain in the 5th century. With regard to Australia, the landmass thought to exist in the southern hemisphere was named *terra australis incognita* or the "unknown southern land".

Closer to home, your blogger has paraphrased the Latin phrase *ergo cogito sum* ("I think, therefore I am") to I think, therefore I blog. Can you believe the audacity of some people? However, it would be unfair to categorise me as *non compos mentis* ("not of sound mind"). I just wanted to incorporate some Latin into my *modus operandi* ("method of operation").

As I have been *in situ* ("in place") as a blogger for almost eight years, I think I can now add that skill to my *curriculum vitae* ("course of one's life"). My online *alter ego* ("the other I") is always challenging the *status quo* ("existing state"), yet he writes *paucis verbis* ("in few words") on each blog topic.

It can be seen that Latin is not the extinct language of the Roman Empire, even though no country today officially speaks it. Latin words and expressions remain ubiquitous in the English language. This is not surprising as the Romans were in Britain for nearly 400 years and left a strong influence on the local speech.

Postscriptum: I apologise for going on *ad infinitum - mea culpa*. But I thought I should add that *postscriptum* is also a Latin word meaning "written after".

Posting Date: 8 February 2016

restoring trust

Perceptions never cease to fascinate me. We see the world not as it is but how we have been conditioned to see it. Take war as an example. There was a protracted conflict in Indochina from 1962-1972. Americans call that Southeast Asian conflict the Vietnam War while the Vietnamese refer to it as the American War.

Same war, different perceptions, and so it is with many things in life. Other people's perceptions are very important, particularly in business. Impressions are made within seconds and - as they say - you never get a second chance to make a first impression.

The most important perceptions in business are customer perceptions. Perception is reality when it comes to customers and their perceptions can be formed from personal experience in dealing with an organisation or from what others say about an organisation (brand reputation).

People value brands that meet their needs and expectations. When you have a favourable interaction with an organisation, you will perceive that as a positive customer experience. Conversely, when your expectations are not met, you will have a negative feeling about a brand.

Negative perceptions put a brand at risk. A recently released global survey by Deloitte identified reputational risk as a top strategic business issue with 88% of executives surveyed. Deloitte also found that customers are the most important stakeholder group when it comes to managing reputational risk.

The *Reputation@Risk* survey revealed that financial services firms view reputation as their greatest risk area. Looking after people's money is serious business which is why banking is built on public trust. Sadly, trust in the banking system plummeted following the Global Financial Crisis (GFC).

Many argue that the GFC was caused by a lack of ethical behaviour. The public perception was that Wall Street looked after itself at the expense of Main Street. Bankers were seen as morally bankrupt, putting their own interests before their customers.

The GFC impacted the day-to-day lives of citizens around the world. Some lost wealth while others lost jobs. Workers were angry that the titans of the financial sector walked away with bucket loads of money while the taxpayer footed the corporate clean-up bill.

There is no doubt that the post-crisis perception of customers to financial institutions is different to the pre-crisis perception. The reputation-battered sector has worked hard to recover its brand equity scores. But consumer trust and confidence will take time to completely rebuild.

At the end of the day, the banking and finance sector is a service industry and reputation is arguably the industry's most valuable asset. For my money, trust and reputation are inseparable which is why some financial institutions have the word trust in their name.

Of course, it requires more than clever branding to have a reputation you can bank on. According to a UK report following the financial crisis, financial institutions must meet three conditions to be perceived as trustworthy:

- COMPETENCE: Provide quality customer service while delivering value to clients and adhering to regulations and legal requirements.

- BENEVOLENCE: Demonstrate due care and concern for the interests of stakeholders by having a positive and not detrimental impact on them.

- INTEGRITY: Adhere to moral, ethical and legal principles and standards, including honesty, fairness and fulfilment of promises.

This sounds like a recipe for success for all businesses, particularly in the digital age, where bad news spreads at the blink of a cursor. In this digital era, customers want their financial institution to be a part of their lives, not just a place for their money.

Posting Date: 8 December 2014

business lessons

Business education is big business. Each year universities around the world turn out thousands of MBA graduates. These budding captains of industry are destined to become tomorrow's business leaders. But are they equipped with the necessary skills to lead?

The Global Financial Crisis (GFC) damaged the reputation of business schools. Some of the best and brightest MBAs contributed to the crisis which plunged the world into deep financial turmoil. Curricula and courses have since been rewritten to ensure that newer graduates don't make the same mistakes.

My sense is that MBA schools became an unofficial scapegoat for the GFC, but this had positive pedagogical implications. Business schools now place a higher emphasis on risk, governance and ethics with the underlying message being that "greed is not good".

MBA degrees cover the science or theory of management. As an MBA graduate, I found the theory very useful and informative. However, as any management theorist will tell you, management is also an art. The term "art" relates to the actual practice of management.

The art of management is learnt on the job in the University of Hard Knocks - the school that rounds-out business education. Having been a management practitioner for over 30 years, I've learned a few things along the way. Please allow me to share three things which I didn't find in management text books.

Kill people with kindness
Contrary to conventional wisdom, you can have a heart and still run a successful business. At the end of the day, business is all about connecting with people. A command and control style doesn't bring out the best in subordinates

and showing compassion is not a sign of weakness. People have a universal need to be respected and that includes employees, suppliers, regulators and other stakeholders. As I stated in my post, *The Power of Nice*, being kind to others is good for business.

Slower is often faster
Everything does not have to be done yesterday and you don't have to be first to blaze a new trail. This certainly applies to product development where first movers are often overtaken by rapid market followers. The constant pressure to deliver instant results has created a business cancer - *short-termism*. As I explained in *Short-term gain, long-term loss*, the GFC was the result of the manic pursuit of quick profits. Both borrowers and lenders saw real estate as an overnight get-rich-quick scheme.

Beware of experts bearing predictions
Virtually no one predicted many of the defining events in modern history including the Great Depression, the Second World War, the fall of the Berlin Wall, the 9/11 terrorists attacks and the Global Financial Crisis. Yet the world is full of people who claim to be an expert at something. While bold predictions make for good headlines, the reality is we cannot even predict the weather or the winner of the Melbourne Cup. My cynicism of seers found expression in my post, *The Certainty of Uncertainty*.

Over and above these three tips, I try in both my professional and personal life to make common sense, common practice. We all intuitively know what we should do in a given situation. A little common sense, particularly in the art of management, goes a long way. You don't need an MBA to implement common sense which is why effective leaders are good at the basics.

Posting Date: 21 May 2012

generational battle

A recently released study on wealth across generations by independent think tank, the Grattan Institute, shows that older Australians are capturing a growing share of Australia's wealth, while the wealth of younger Australians has stagnated. The report, *The Wealth of Generations*, finds that Gen Y may be the first generation ever to be less wealthy than that of their parents.

Baby boomers have benefited greatly from the boom in housing prices over the past two decades. Gen Yers - with lower and falling rates of home ownership - have shared less of this huge windfall. Across all household age categories, housing accounts for around half of the average wealth and older Australians hold more property (by value) and therefore more wealth.

Beyond capital gains, the report notes that over the period 2004-2010, incomes grew fastest for older Australians, allowing them to add more to their wealth by saving. Also, governments are spending much more on older households for pensions and services, particularly health. The report goes on to say the next generation will be worse off unless governments act:

> Targeting the Age Pension, reducing superannuation tax concessions and shifting towards asset taxes could reduce the transfers between today's younger taxpayers and older retirees. These reforms would fall most on those who have benefited from windfalls, government largesse, and paying lower taxes while deficits accumulated.

The Grattan Institute claims that "young Australians (are) set to pay for government policy mistakes". It seems that many financial journalists agree writing supportive articles under emotive headlines such as *"The fiscal storm confronting young Australia"* and *"Baby boomers prosper at (the) expense of the young"* and *"Generation Y have every right to be angry"*.

Personally, I think it's a bit rich to blame one generation for the plight of another. It's also cut-and-dry to suggest that only older Australians benefit from tax concessions. Not to be forgotten in this debate is the fact that only a small percentage of retirees receive the age pension and that many older Australians live in poverty.

Tim Costello, the Baptist minister and chief executive of World Vision Australia, had a more philosophical reaction to the Grattan Report. He acknowledged that throughout history parents have made incredible sacrifices to give their children a better life than their own. But he thinks it's time for a reality check as we may have lost perspective in giving our kids too much:

> Today if your kids have to share a bedroom, it's as if it's a denial of their fundamental human rights. That's the nonsense we've got to. Today we have both sides of politics telling people who live in McMansions with two cars, 'You're a victim. Your electricity price has gone up. You're in struggle town.' We really have lost the plot.

Another voice of reason in this emotive debate is Emily Millane. She wrote an article for *The Drum* in which she pointed out that variances within each generation are where the real policy complexities and solutions to social inequalities lie. "So variable is the wealth within generations," wrote Millane, "that it's far more useful ... to understand the real dividing line in our society (is) class."

In contrast to the Grattan Institute, another Australian think tank, The Centre for Independent Studies, believes we need a more informed and balanced debate about tax concessions.

In a recent article - *Rorts for the rich are a myth* - a senior fellow at The Centre argued that dumping tax breaks on super and capital gains will not save anything like the critics claim. However, their removal would certainly damage saving and investing.

As I have acknowledged before in this blog, economic inequality is real and can be excessive. But pitting Gen Yers against baby boomers in tit-for-tat arguments - such as trading blows over housing - is not helpful. Baby boomers argue that they paid 17% on their mortgages in the late 1980s. Gen Yers counter by pointing out that mortgage rates may be lower today but so is housing affordability (i.e., the cost of a home relative to income).

The growing wealth gap between young and old is a worldwide phenomenon. As I outlined in *Income inequality*, seven out of ten people live in countries where economic inequality has increased in the last 30 years. Government policy choices in areas such as taxation can help address inequality. But disproportionate wealth gains will always be part and parcel of free-market societies.

Posting Date: 3 March 2015

population debate

We find it difficult to have a rational debate in Australia about population. The arguments for and against a larger population are often ill-informed. On both sides, emotionally charged claims and counter-claims unnecessarily polarise the community. The debate needs to be reframed to find solutions to the real problem - an aging population.

The proportion of Australians over 65 will grow to 25% of the population by 2050, up from 13%. This prediction was made in the Government's third *Intergenerational Report*, released early last year. Unfortunately, the report captured the public's attention for another reason - its prediction that Australia's population will grow to 36 million by 2050.

This headline grabbing figure has overshadowed the more important debate about the fall in the labour force participation rate. Whereas in 2010 we had five people of working age to every person 65 and over, this ratio is expected to fall to just 2.7 workers in 2050 to every retiree. This is a scary number as proportionally there will be fewer taxpayers working to support older Australians.

In any country, the key drivers of economic growth are population size, workplace participation rates and productivity levels (the three Ps). An increase in any one or more of these factors leads to economic growth and improved economic prosperity. A well-managed immigration program contributes to all three of these factors.

Immigration accounts for two-thirds of Australia's population growth and migrants to our shores are mostly of prime working age. As noted by the Department of Immigration, migrants add to the labour force, lower the age profile of the population, increase workplace participation rates and add to productivity.

Of course, there are many who reject the economic need argument for immigration and say we just can't sustain a bigger population. These individuals are understandably concerned that governments might not be up to the task of providing energy, water and transport infrastructure for rapidly growing cities.

But a leading Australian academic, Professor Peter McDonald, says that migrants should not be used as scapegoats for the failures of public planning. Successive waves of post-war migration have expanded our capacity as a nation and created the prosperity we now enjoy. If we had waited for governments to firstly put in the necessary infrastructure, we would be a backwater today.

At the end of the day, it may well be that politicians can do very little about population growth. According to a recently released report, a bigger Australia is as certain as death and taxes. "It is wrong to think we can control Australia's population size by simply cutting migration," the report says.

Japan has the world's oldest population and its on-going economic woes provide a sobering lesson. Japan's aging and declining population is severely impacting domestic demand. Worse still, Japan is heading for a permanent state of economic malaise with its population expected to shrink from 128 million to 90 million by 2050.

Just as no company can massively scale back its investment in people and simply let its workforce age, the same holds true for nations. Size does matter, which is why I'm a fan of a big Australia and want to avoid what one academic has called The Small Australia Nightmare. A smaller Australia means bigger taxes and higher interest rates. I certainly don't want that - do you?

Posting Date: 7 February 2011

planning myths

It's that time of year when many organisations are turning their attention to strategic planning. This time-honoured annual ritual requires organisations to gather their top lieutenants together, lock them in a room and then come out with a sacred document called a strategic plan.

A strategic plan is often seen as a panacea to the myriad challenges facing an organisation. However, a plan does not of itself automatically produce results. The perfect plan is useless unless it is implemented. Strategy is not just about planning - it's also about doing.

Planning is a critical component of good management and governance. It creates a roadmap for organisational direction and decision making. But many so-called strategic plans are just a laundry list of operational projects which lack the 'ah-ha' X-factor of new strategic ideas and initiatives.

When done well, strategic planning can help troubled organisations succeed and move successful organisations to the next level of performance. Most plans, however, deliver far less than expected and the root cause of this lies in the actual planning process itself.

Strategic planning has been defined as "the science of making good decisions about the future". These decisions are typically made at the annual, offsite planning conference. Much of the conventional wisdom about how these conferences should be run and what they can achieve is, I believe, misplaced.

I've lost count of how many strategic planning workshops I've attended in my career. I've also facilitated quite a number of planning sessions. From this experience I know that many planning workshops fall foul of some classic misconceptions, two of which I have outlined below.

Myth 1: Group consensus equals success. A planning conference is not a love-in where participants are meant to agree on everything. Robust debate and discussion is the key to achieving strategic breakthroughs. Yet many people within a planning group are unwilling to rock the boat.

This creates steady-as-she-goes thinking rather than state-of-the-art thinking and occurs due to a phenomenon called groupthink. Groupthink drives members of a group to seek consensus or unanimity at the cost of considering alternate courses of action.

Groupthink leads to intelligent and knowledgeable individuals making poor decisions as part of a group. In the interests of cohesiveness, people conform to group norms and are reluctant to think outside the square. Playing the devil's advocate is frowned upon.

Myth 2: Planning can be done in a day. Strategic planning is not a singular event - it is a never ending process. The future, by definition, always faces us, so organisations must always be in the simultaneous process of planning and implementing their plans.

With regard to the actual planning workshop, you need to plan before you plan. You can't arrive at an offsite planning workshop without having done your homework. A successful strategic planning workshop requires lots of preparatory work and thought.

Innovative ideas can't be forced and strategies cannot be conceived on demand. Most strategies emerge over time rather than being deliberately planned at a single point in time. No organisation exists in a static environment which is why strategies must be free to appear at any time.

Against this background, Gateway is holding its 2013

strategic planning conference this Saturday and I'm looking forward to some robust debate. We intend to challenge some sacred cows as business-as-usual is not a viable option given our rapidly changing operating environment.

I suspect Gateway's planning team will be out of its comfort zone throughout the day. We will encourage diverse voices and will not settle for the lowest common denominator that everyone can live with. Rather, we will strive for solutions that challenge our current thinking and deliver the greatest benefit to members. Our member-owners expect nothing less.

Posting Date: 11 March 2013

higher purpose

Last week I named my blog, Doubting Thomas. I explained the philosophical connections to this new name and its link to critical thinking. Given my blog's new moniker, you might be expecting me to write something deep and meaningful this week. After all, philosophers (descendants of Plato) are meant to tackle the big issues of life.

I toyed briefly with offering a view on ethics, metaphysics and logic, but thought that might be too esoteric. So, I turned my attention to the philosophy of economics and moral questions concerning welfare, justice and freedom. It then struck me that contemporary economic theory is about rational choice, so I decided that should be my focus for this week.

[Note to reader: What constitutes a rational choice for one individual might be irrational for another. When making a decision, each individual, according to rational choice theory, will weigh the likely positive benefits against likely negative consequences and then base their choice on what they think will ultimately benefit them the most.]

My next dilemma was to work out how to best explain rational choice and to provide an example which overlaid socio-economic factors such as lifestyle and the influence of others on the decisions we make. After some pondering - which is what philosophers do - I recalled the classic story of *The Businessman and the Fisherman*. I have reproduced the story below.

Unfortunately, I don't know the identity of the author. For me, the moral of the story is about understanding what you truly want out of life and what matters most to you. Often what we want is right under our noses, we just don't know it! I hope you enjoy the story as part of your own pursuit of happiness and wisdom.

Once upon a time ... an American businessman was standing at the pier of a small coastal Mexican village when a small boat with just one fisherman docked. Inside the small boat were several large yellow-fin tuna. The American complimented the Mexican on the quality of his fish.

"How long did it take you to catch them?" the American inquired.

"Only a little while," the Mexican replied.

"Why don't you stay out longer and catch more fish?" the American then asked.

"I have enough to support my family's immediate needs," the Mexican explained.

"But," the American persisted, "what do you do with the rest of your time?"

The Mexican fisherman said, "I sleep late, fish a little, play with my children, take a siesta with my wife, Maria, stroll into the village each evening where I sip wine and play guitar with my amigos. I have a full and busy life, senor."

The American scoffed, "I am a Harvard MBA and can help you. You should spend more time fishing and with the proceeds buy a bigger boat, and with the proceeds from the bigger boat you could buy several boats. Eventually you would have a fleet of fishing boats."

The Harvard hotshot continued. "Instead of selling your catch to a middleman you would sell directly to consumers, eventually opening your own cannery. You would control the product, processing and distribution. Of course, you would need to leave this small coastal fishing village and move to Mexico City, then LA and eventually NYC where you will run your expanding enterprise."

The Mexican fisherman asked, "But senor, how long will this all take?"

To which the American replied, "15-20 years."

"But what then, senor?"

The American laughed and exclaimed, "That's the best part! When the time is right you would announce an IPO (Initial Public Offering) and sell your company stock to the public and become very rich. You would make millions."

"Millions, senor? Then what?"

The American said slowly, "Then you would retire, move to a small coastal fishing village where you would sleep late, fish a little, play with your kids, take a siesta with your wife, Maria, stroll to the village in the evenings where you could sip wine and play your guitar with your amigos..."

Posting Date: 1 April 2013

chaos theory

Believe it or not, there's a scientific theory (chaos theory) which posits that when a butterfly flaps its wings in Brazil it can set off a tornado in Texas. This is known as the butterfly effect - a term attributed to Edward Lorenz - and it's become a popular metaphor to describe how tiny and seemingly insignificant events can have large and far-reaching consequences.

The "flapping wing" can be just one driver whose careless actions cause a traffic jam for thousands of other motorists. It can be a mutating virus in African monkeys which creates a thunderstorm for humanity in the form of AIDS. Or it can be a decline in the number of pollinating honey bees resulting in a multi-billion dollar impact on the fruit and vegetable industries.

Nature has always been global and now the globalisation of trade and finance means the butterfly effect is everywhere at work. In an interdependent world, a drought in Australia can cause a shortage of rice in Haiti, a financial debacle in Greece can threaten Swiss banks and toxic US sub-prime mortgages can unleash a Global Financial Crisis (GFC).

Small mistakes can also cause big problems in organisations. One bad customer experience can result in a consumer avoiding your product for life. One disgruntled team member can poison an entire culture. In business, every action affects another as everything is connected.

The corollary of the butterfly effect is that you can achieve big results through small actions. Individual households recycling waste help create a better world. A random act of kindness has a ripple effect on those around you. One employee can spark a conversation that fuels a thought which changes how an organisation is run.

The butterfly effect found mass appeal with the publication in 1988 of James Gleick's bestseller, *Chaos: Making a New*

Science. Chaos is the science of surprises. It teaches us to expect the unexpected. Chaos theory deals with nonlinear, complex systems that are impossible to predict or control such as weather patterns, water flows, financial markets and organisations.

The essence of chaos is something called "sensitive dependence on initial conditions". Dynamic systems are highly dependent on their initial conditions. The slightest difference in initial conditions - even beyond the human ability to measure such differences - can produce vastly different outcomes. Some examples will help here.

Two paper boats placed side-by-side on a river will follow different routes and end up in different places as each will be subject to small variations in force. Similarly, a group of helium balloons launched together will eventually land in different places. Thus, a tiny deviation in initial conditions will generate diverging outcomes.

In economics, small changes can also magnify into large scale macro changes. Markets are dynamic and unpredictable which is why the GFC came as a complete surprise to economists. Economists failed to spot the most destructive financial shock since the Great Depression and this was a humbling experience for economic forecasters.

Economists are trained to believe that markets are "deterministic systems". In other words, they are predictable systems in which cause and effect are discernible. In reality, markets are "nonlinear systems" characterised by unpredictable behaviour.

The GFC clearly demonstrated that we humans are far too emotive for rational economic models to accurately predict our behaviour. In the pursuit of financial gain, many lenders, borrowers and investors did not act rationally. When the subprime bubble burst, markets tanked, people panicked and emotions took over.

It can be seen that small, wing-flapping events can create true hurricane-sized changes. As individuals, as workers and as consumers, the little things we do matter. Big might be beautiful but small is mighty. It's the power of one and we can all make a difference.

Posting Date: 15 February 2016

risk assessment

We all face a multitude of risks in our daily lives. Each of us is exposed to personal risk (e.g., injury) and collective risk (e.g., terrorism). Some risks are forced upon us (emergency surgery) while others are undertaken by choice (air travel).

We can take legal risks (gambling), health risks (smoking), sporting risks (parachuting) and hygiene risks (shaving). Some risks are predictable (drugs) while others are unforeseeable (tsunami).

Given all the risks around us you might be forgiven for not wanting to get out of bed - but that poses its own set of risks! Just as risk is an inescapable part of life, it's also inherent in everything a business does or does not do.

It's impossible to run a business without taking risks. Indeed, it's unhealthy to even try as you'll risk stagnation. Companies which can see beyond risks to the opportunities they present are much more likely to prosper.

The process of identifying, assessing and managing risks is known as risk management. Following the Global Financial Crisis (GFC), banking regulators around the world have understandably put the spotlight on risk management and this is a good thing.

Organisations which are effective at managing risk have developed risk-based organisational cultures where staff and managers instinctively look for risks. The same broad principles apply to households which should also put in place strategies to mitigate risks.

For most Australians their home is their biggest asset and needs to be protected against the risk of damage. But our greatest asset - particularly for younger people - is the ability to generate an income.

Income risk arising from the loss of a job or inability to work due to disability is real. Yet only 35% of Australians have insurance to protect against the severe financial distress caused by a loss of income.

On the other side of the ledger, we also face expense risk. Life has a way of throwing up unexpected bills and this risk can be mitigated by having an emergency fund to cover sudden expenses.

Another risk that all of us will face at some time is retirement risk. If you don't put away sufficient money into superannuation, you'll run the real risk of outliving your retirement savings.

From time-to-time it's important to step back and reassess the risks in our lives. This risk assessment forms part of life planning. Remember, while no one plans to fail, many people just fail to plan.

Posting Date: 11 April 2011

winning performance

London is the only city to host the Olympic Games three times. The first was in 1908, the second time was in 1948 and the third London Olympics will begin this Friday. The Games of the XXX Olympiad will see 205 nations represented by 10,500 athletes take part in 302 medal events.

During 19 days of competition across 26 sports the crème de la crème of international athletes will battle for Olympic Gold. In doing so, they will encapsulate the Olympic motto *'Citius, Altius, Fortius'* which is Latin for Faster, Higher, Stronger.

Only the best-of-the-best will get to stand on the winner's dais. Each will have produced an exceptional performance and their success will have come only after years of sacrifice. Those who reach the top of their sport have focus, stamina, determination and a never say die attitude.

Business is also a very competitive game and sport provides lessons that transfer to the boardroom and executive office. Indeed, sport is a powerful metaphor for business and there are some striking parallels. In both arenas one must set goals, work hard, visualize success and strive for peak performance.

Peak performance is defined as the ability of an individual, group, team or organisation to perform at a consistently high level for a sustained period of time. Finding ways to create and sustain peak levels of performance is a challenge every business leader faces.

In my experience, peak performers are single-minded in their pursuit of excellence and success. They are self-reliant and thrive under pressure. For an organisation to reach peak performance, every employee must be committed to achieving their individual goals which, in turn, contribute to accomplishing the organisation's overall strategic objectives.

Creating this alignment falls to the leadership team within each organisation. Organisational leaders must be able to lead, motivate and articulate a clear vision. Their primary goal is to unleash the potential in every employee. But employees must also be prepared to work together.

Teamwork is one of the basic skills required in the workplace. Just as no sports team can win if everyone is not pulling in the same direction, the same holds true in the corporate world. The "Lone Ranger" persona must give way to the belief that "none of us is as good as all of us".

Invariably, to reach our goals we need the help and co-operation of others. Being a team player calls for collaboration. A team within an organisation is more than just a group of people - it's a group of individuals who believe in achieving a common goal.

In London, the Aussie Olympic team will have a single focus - to do their best and to represent Australia proudly. At Gateway, we too pull together to build stronger outcomes for the business. Each Gateway team member has unique skills and abilities and everyone has a contribution to make.

As Gateway's head coach, my job is to improve the performance of the team, both collectively as a group and as individuals. This requires a genuine passion and real desire to help people grow and develop in order to reach their full potential.

The Olympic Creed states: *"The most important thing in the Olympic Games is not to win but to take part, just as the most important thing in life is not the triumph but the struggle. The essential thing is not to have conquered but to have fought well."*

At Gateway, we "fight well" every day.

Posting Date: 23 July 2012

national optimism

With the festive season rapidly approaching and the year drawing to a close, it's appropriate to reflect on the year that was. Despite all the geopolitical gloom and doom that has dominated the headlines during 2014, we are still here. The world has not been engulfed by global conflict, financial systems have not collapsed and society has not experienced economic Armageddon.

While it's true we still don't have peace on Earth and our planet is battling the deadly Ebola virus, we do have cause for optimism. Around the world, wealth is rising, poverty is falling and environmental issues are on the agenda. As philosopher, Tim Dean, noted in a recent article: "...the world is becoming a safer, richer and generally better place to live" as each year passes.

Why are we so negative? Why do many of us see the glass as half-empty? Well, we humans like bad news more than good news. The news is a form of entertainment and there's nothing more entertaining than drama. That's what drives the fear-mongering media and their stories about housing bubbles, economic downturns and a debt apocalypse.

According to US President, Barack Obama, the media is dominated by reporting about conflicts, disasters and problems. He made this remark during his recent visit to Australia as part of the G20 Leaders' Forum in Brisbane while delivering an address at the University of Queensland. During that speech he called for optimism, saying:

> Never in the history of humanity have people lived longer, are they more likely to be healthy, more likely to be enjoying basic security ... opportunities are limitless for this generation. You are living in an extraordinary time.

Regular readers of this blog know that I'm not a fan of naysayers. To be frank, I don't understand pessimists. Sadly, the world is full of people who expect the worst. Yet the physical, emotional and economic benefits of having a positive mental attitude are well documented.

It shouldn't be hard to be positive in Australia. As a nation, we are enjoying our 23rd year of continuous annual GDP growth - a feat unmatched in our history. Also, according to investment bank, Credit Suisse, Australians are the richest people in the world.

In October, the Swiss bank released the results of its fifth annual study of global wealth trends. Our love affair with real estate propelled Aussies to the top of the rich list with a median wealth per Australian adult of $US225,000. Belgium took second place, well back on $US173,000.

Not only do we punch above our weight in terms of wealth, we also do very well compared to other nations in a range of areas including longevity, education and health. Australia's position as one of the best places in the world to live was confirmed in the latest UN Human Development Report.

The 2014 Report places Australia second behind Norway for human development. Australia has ranked in the top five nations on the UN's Human Index Rating since 1998. Our quality of life is the envy of the world yet many of us do not see the Land of Oz as the lucky country.

My wish in this season of goodwill is that we better appreciate this great democracy of ours. We can speak our minds without fear of reprisal and we can worship without fear of persecution as the human rights of all Australian citizens are protected by the rule of law.

We are free to make choices. I choose to be a proud and optimistic Aussie. I choose to rise above media scaremongering, political infighting and alarmist doomsayers. I choose to acknowledge our achievements as a nation. I choose - in the words of our national anthem - to "Advance Australia Fair"!

Posting Date: 15 December 2014

beyond borders

Dear Earthlings,

Allow me to introduce myself. My name is Zork and I've just arrived from planet Mars. Due to a navigational error I landed in Paul Thomas' backyard and he has been proudly educating me about life on Earth.

Given what Paul has told me, I find it hard to believe you are the most intelligent life form on this planet. As a well-travelled alien explorer, I believe your behaviour is light years from how a civilised society should act.

You inhabit an extraordinarily beautiful planet. Yet you have artificially divided it into 194 sovereign nations and this is the root cause of many of your world's problems.

You act selfishly as citizens of independent nation-states instead of behaving selflessly as one united global family. By viewing the world through national-interest glasses, you fail to clearly see and deal with global issues.

Your planet's Great Depression is an example of this parochial thinking. After the 1929 stock market crash, nation-states sheltered their domestic industries from international competition and this led to a collapse in global demand.

Your recent Global Financial Crisis again showed you live in a borderless world. No country was immune from its effects even though some threatened to escape behind protectionist trade barriers - history repeating itself!

Just as the great oceans you navigate and the air you breathe know no national boundaries, so it is in a global economy. The challenge humanity faces is to better manage an interdependent world.

You must evolve beyond a world order built around

the sovereign state system. Rest assured, however, that successful global governance does not require a monolithic global government.

What is needed is a change in mindset to facilitate true global co-operation and consensus. To paraphrase your great leader, John F. Kennedy, you should ask not what the world can do for you but what you can do for the world.

Let me conclude with a general observation. In the cosmic scheme of things, the Earth is just a baby in size and age, yet you *Homo sapiens* act as if you are the centre of the universe.

If the 4.5 billion years of your planet's existence was compressed into a single year, modern humans would make an appearance on Earth at three seconds to midnight on 31 December.

You haven't even roamed the Earth for as long as the dinosaurs - you still have much to learn. So, be nice to each other and be kind to your environment. I have enormous faith in your ability to become a great people and to live in peace and harmony. Best wishes from Zork.

Posting Date: 3 May 2010

resource efficiency

On a number of occasions I have used this blog to conduct book reviews. I mainly critique business and finance literature but have appraised tomes from other genres including health and well-being. I cast a broad, non-fiction reading net as the writings which impact the business world do not fit neatly into one discipline.

For each book I review, I outline its major underlying themes or concepts. My blog word count limit does not allow me to conduct an in-depth description and evaluation of the author's thesis. Given this, I invariably omit facets that could be the subject of another blog post or three.

Well this week, for the very first time, I'd like to write a second post about a book I've already assessed - *The Sixth Wave*. The book contains a very interesting chapter on changing business models which I didn't mention in my original review. So let me do that now - but first, a quick reminder of what *The Sixth Wave* is about.

The book's premise is that we have been through five waves of change since the Industrial Revolution and are about to experience a sixth wave of innovation. Resource efficiency is at the heart of this sixth wave and will see companies eliminate waste by selling services, not products. The authors predict the shift from product to service "...will change the face of commerce".

The mobile phone is a good example of a product that is now marketed as a service, making it far more profitable. Mobile phones are very expensive. When phone companies realised the real value was not in the hardware but in the service - the actual phone call - they started giving away the handset.

Other industries are now joining the shift from a product

to a service focus as they increasingly understand that (i) the things we consume are different to the things we use and (ii) waste equals opportunity. The authors provide some mind-expanding examples and reveal a new economic model that rewards sustainability.

For instance, the authors view a car as an "incredibly costly resource (that) spends most of its life sitting idle .... A more sensible approach would be to have a car (only) when you need it". They foresee an increasing number of drivers using car sharing services like GoGet.

With GoGet you pay for the service the car provides - transportation and mobility - rather than for the car itself (i.e., the product). GoGet benefits not only members but also the environment. It's claimed that one shared car can take seven privately owned vehicles off the road thereby reducing congestion and pollution.

Another example of a company trying to reduce its ecological footprint is carpet manufacturer, Interface, which now rents carpet. Clients like it because it's easier on their cashflow. Interface profits from pricing its rented carpet tiles to reflect true value to the consumer. And the environment benefits as Interface ensures proper recycling - so much less carpet ends up in landfill.

In the same vein, the authors argue that less car tyres would end up in landfill if they were also rented. "Selling tyre services," they say, "...would create an incentive for manufacturers to develop a tyre that would last for 200,000 kilometres rather than 50,000 kilometres."

The boundaries between products and services are also blurring with regard to energy which too can be viewed as a service. People do not want to "...own litres of oil, tonnes of coal or megawatts of electricity". Rather, they seek the services that fuel enables - heat, light and mobility. UK energy-services company, Thameswey, has designed its business models around selling energy services rather than energy. It really is a brave new world!

Posting Date: 23 May 2011

futurist's forecasts

Unless your name is Nostradamus, anytime you make predictions you run the risk of looking foolish. This hasn't stopped Frenchman, Jacques Attali, offering a raft of brave and controversial predictions for the 21st century in his book, *A Brief History of the Future*.

While Attali's book is a good read, I challenge its accuracy. This modern day soothsayer is trying to predict a whopping 100 years into the future and I don't think that's possible.

In 1966 TIME magazine published an essay, *Looking Toward A.D. 2000*, which utterly failed to predict what our world would be like at the start of the new millennium. Just as there are no freeways in the sky today (another false prediction!) I struggle to believe there will be no governments in 2100 - but that's Attali's view.

He argues that "money will finally rid itself of everything that threatens it - including nation-states". Attali foresees a borderless world governed by ultra-liberal market forces. Even as a proud capitalist, the idea of sovereign states giving way to a "super empire" co-ordinated by huge corporations frightens me.

The Global Financial Crisis has shown that governments have an important role to play in markets. The world would have suffered financial calamity had it not been for the speed and united interventions of policy makers.

Attali's prospective look at the next 50 years includes the decline of the American Empire (he predicts by 2035). But it's his retrospective assessment of human history I find instructive.

As someone with a keen interest in human history, I know it's based on three interlocking stories: religion, war and commerce. In the same vein, Attali argues that since the dawn of time "three powers have always coexisted: the religious ... the military ... and the mercantile".

He goes on to say that each of these three dominant powers has controlled wealth. "Turn by turn, the master becomes the slave, the soldier replaces the priest, the merchant replaces the soldier."

In terms of political orders, humanity started with the *ritual order*, progressed to the *imperial order* and has moved to the *mercantile order*. It is this mercantile order which Attali predicts will be replaced by a unified and stateless global market - a "super empire".

Apparently, the super empire will be controlled by an elite class of selfish people called "hyper-nomads". It is the "nomadisation" process - caused by the decentralising power of the Internet and the mobility of high-tech nomadic workers - which will make nation-states irrelevant.

For my money, I hope I'm not around when the hyper-nomads rule the Earth. I'll leave it to you to decide whether Attali's views are science fact or science fiction.

Posting Date: 14 September 2009

blog milestone

Eight years ago this week, I held my breath, took the plunge and launched my blogging career. To be precise, it was on the morning of 25 March 2008 that I hit "publish" on my very first blog post. Little did I know that that initial post would be followed (to date) by another 360 posts.

I truly thought that I would quickly run out of steam and that my life as a blogger would be short-lived. As it transpired, my creative well did not run dry. I have been able to push through the occasional writer's block to publish new content every week without fail.

Blogging has taken my life in a direction I never expected - that of an author. My CEO Blog has spawned one book with another on the way. Blogging has also helped me in my role as a CEO. Writing a weekly post has forced me to keep up with contemporary issues which impact Gateway and its members.

My penchant for less government regulation - lest we become a Nanny State - has found expression in a number of my posts. Around the world, freedoms are being replaced by constraints. *Laissez-faire* is being suffocated by red tape and bureaucracy as regulation runs amok, intruding into our everyday lives.

My frustration at our almost hysterical response to government debt has also been a recurring theme of my posts. Nobel prize-winning economist, Joseph Stiglitz, argues that deficit spending, when done right, can be a major stimulus to economic growth and can actually lower long-term government debt.

Something else that has been the subject of repeated commentary in my blog is the grey tsunami sweeping the world. Population aging is real and has far-reaching social and economic consequences. I'm yet to be convinced that we truly understand the ramifications of this demographic megatrend.

Not to be forgotten among my pet topics over recent years is the impact of technology on our lives. Technology is a double-edged sword which can be both a boon and bane for society. I am neither Luddite nor Evangelist when it comes to technology. I embrace technology, but refuse to let it rule my life.

As a blogger, I was once accused of being a "fence-sitter". I learned very early in my blogging career that readers want to hear my opinion. After publishing a post in early 2010 on climate change, I received (justifiable) criticism from a reader for not taking a clear position in the debate.

Nowadays, my posts resemble discursive essays that (hopefully) present a balanced examination of a subject. I do my best to outline both sides of every argument, letting the facts and details speak for themselves. However, I do offer a concluding opinion on each topic so that my readers know where I stand.

Writing for you over the past eight years has been a joy and privilege. You have helped me find my voice and given me a forum to express my views on the issues that are shaping politics, redesigning business, changing society and driving technology.

Each blog anniversary is a milestone. As I blow out the candles on my eight-year anniversary cake, I move into my ninth year as a blogger with renewed vigour. I am gratified and humbled at the number of people who follow my blog and thank you for clicking on each week.

Posting Date: 21 March 2016

shelving retirement

A baby born in Australia in 1908 had a life expectancy of 57 years. Today, the life expectancy of Australians has hit an average of 81.4 years, second only to Japan. Having survived to age 65, life expectancy is higher than at birth - men can expect to live another 18.3 years and women another 21.5 years. Based on these figures, retirement for many baby boomers will not be a five-year sprint but a 20 plus year marathon.

A life of leisure might sound appealing but what about purpose and meaning? Happiness in retirement is about being active and for some this purposeful activity will take the form of work. The authors of *Avoid Retirement and Stay Alive* believe that the longer you work the longer you live. Research shows that almost 20% of baby boomers plan never to retire.

While success in retirement is about much more than the money, it does not mean you can ignore the question: How much do I need to retire? The answer to this will be influenced by your choice of retirement age.

Like 50% of full-time workers in their fifties, I plan never to retire. When the corporate world tells me my time is up, I'll finish writing the book I've been (slowly) working on, possibly do more study and then maybe lecture. My dad is in his mid-seventies and still works, albeit part time, just to keep himself active.

I have absolutely no intention of sitting in a rocking chair on the porch. I don't want to be part of a granny state but an active state of mind.

Posting Date: 14 July 2008

04
Technological Advances

▪ ▪ Chapter Overview

Technology is rapidly changing and expanding in every field. The gadget-filled 21st century is replete with iPhones, Kindles, laptops, tablets and electronic wallets. Technology - particularly the Internet - has transformed how we shop, how we pay for things and how we communicate. People are connected and empowered as never before with gadgets that are slimmer, faster and more energy efficient. In this penultimate chapter we look at, *inter alia*, the rise of artificial intelligence, the explosion in apps, the introduction of driverless cars, the use of wearable technology and the move to cloud computing.

automated world

There's a raft of technology experts predicting that homes around the world are set to become smarter over the next decade. Using smart appliances connected to the Internet, curtains will close automatically when it's dark, lights will come on at pre-determined times and air conditioners will self-activate to achieve desired temperatures.

An almost endless list of connected devices can now be programmed to respond autonomously to environmental changes. It's part of a new wave of technology called the Internet of Things. The Internet of Things (or IoT) refers to the connection of everyday objects to the Internet and to one another and its application extends way beyond your home.

Imagine a world where sensors on public garbage bins signal they are full and parking spaces let you know when they are occupied. Using this same technology, energy companies will be able to read electricity metres remotely. The IoT will also enable machines on a factory floor to communicate automatically with each other to solve production line problems.

According to Cisco, there will be 50 billion Internet connected things in the world by 2020. It's claimed the IoT will "connect the unconnected", creating unprecedented value for society. The IoT is increasing the connectedness of people and things on a scale that once was unimaginable with connected devices now outnumbering the world's population by 1.5 to 1.

The IoT has been variously described as "machine to machine technology" and "communication among physical objects". Techopedia defines the Internet of Things as "a computing concept that describes a future where every day physical objects will be connected to the Internet and be able to identify themselves to other devices".

It's about adding connectivity and intelligence to just about every device in order to give them special functions. Put simply, devices will be able to talk and work in sync and make autonomous decisions. For example, smart cars will be able to warn you if another car is getting too close and inform you of the best route to avoid traffic jams.

When it comes to banking, the IoT is seen as a natural fit as the delivery of financial services increasingly involves the Internet. Deployment of products like wireless connected ATMs and video enabled financial self-service kiosks are predicted. It is also forecast that mobile phones will replace payment cards and Internet based peer-to-peer lending will become commonplace.

Over and above this, the future of banking is all about data. Internet connected devices are generating vast amounts of information about our behaviours and preferences. Financial institutions will increasingly use this "Big Data" to analyse our past purchases to predict future needs. Welcome to the world of predictive banking which is based on insight, not hindsight.

The IoT may be the next frontier in computing, but is it a solution in search of a problem? Will ambient technology make home life easier? Do I really need an Internet-enabled fridge that identifies when stocks run low and orders more of my favourite goodies? Frankly, my home is not complex so I don't need an app to run the dishwasher, pre-heat the oven or turn on the TV.

I maintain a blog, I tweet, I use an iPhone and I have a laptop, so I'm certainly not a Luddite. But the Doubting Thomas in me knows the dangers of being swept up in the hype surrounding new technology. Technology often over promises and under delivers as expectations lose touch with reality. I'm still waiting for my flying car, robot maid, paperless office and personal jetpack.

My sense is that I'll be manually turning my home lights on and off for quite some time. Also, I prefer my traditional house keys to a remote smart-lock device which can be hacked. And I'm deliberately trying to delay the day when my digital toothbrush alerts my dentist's iPhone that I'm not brushing properly. Perhaps I'm not quite ready for Big Brother!

Posting Date: 16 February 2015

artificial intelligence

Renowned cosmologist, Stephen Hawking, is worried. Microsoft founder, Bill Gates, is worried. Apple co-founder, Steve Wozniak, is worried. Artificial intelligence - in the form of machines that can think - is worrying many people. What was once science fiction - machines smarter than humans - is now becoming science fact.

Professor Hawking and dozens of other luminaries from the scientific and technology communities recently signed an open letter highlighting the potential dangers of artificial intelligence. They warn that without proper safeguards, the rapid growth of artificial intelligence could end in disaster for humanity.

The threat of robot uprising (aka cybernetic revolt) used to be confined to sci-fi movies like *The Terminator*. Now, advances in technology mean it's possible - at least in theory - that life could imitate art. The concern is that by giving computers more and more power we are building machines that may one day outwit us.

Artificial intelligence (AI) is the design of intelligent systems and machines. It gives computers the ability to think, learn and adapt. In manufacturing, machines have long been used to perform boring and/or dangerous jobs. Around the home, sophisticated alarm systems can now observe a monitored environment and "learn" what is normal in order to detect threats.

AI is all around us and is creeping into our daily lives. Most of the AI we interact with is software running in Internet services or apps on our phones and tablets. This AI is bringing human intelligence to everyday technologies. Examples include intelligent systems that recognise our voice commands, correct our spelling and suggest book choices.

My sense is that the labels we put on AI can influence whether it is perceived as friendly or frightening. I don't know anyone who is scared of a MACHINE (like a car or a plane). But if we call something a ROBOT (conjuring up images of the Battle Droids in *Star Wars*) it can evoke fears of silicone and binary humanoids gaining control over flesh and bone humans.

AI helps us drive cars and fly planes. In the medical field, surgical robots are assisting doctors to perform more accurate and less evasive procedures. In banking, financial institutions are embracing "fuzzy logic" in credit scoring systems. This enables a computer to notionally approve or decline a loan based on multiple factors with different levels of importance.

It can be seen that AI has many beneficial uses. So, should we really be worried about the potential downsides? Some argue that if computers develop superhuman intelligence they will be superior to us. Well possibly, but machines with cognitive computing power have been able to beat humans for some time.

In 1997, Deep Blue, a computer built by IBM, defeated world champion chess player, Garry Kasparov. More recently, another IBM built computer - Watson - beat two former champions of the TV game show, *Jeopardy!* Every day, the algorithms that power computers and give them their "electronic brains" to make decisions behind the scenes, are getting smarter.

There is no doubt that the gap between computer intelligence and human intelligence is closing. According to a "theory" posited by AI futurologist, Ray Kurzweil, called singularity, AI will overtake human thinking by 2029. When this tipping point is reached, human biology and intelligent machines will merge into a super-intelligent reality - the singularity.

The Doubting Thomas in me finds it hard to embrace this science fiction sounding prediction of humanity merging with technology. Nonetheless, many "experts" believe it will become reality. For me, this whole debate calls into question what it means to be human. While a machine may be able to swiftly perform mathematical calculations, humans have a gut instinct that can't be replicated via algorithms.

Kurzweil claims that by 2029, AI will enable smart machines to crack jokes, tell stories and learn continuously. But can you teach a computer common sense? Can you give a machine a moral compass? Can robots display empathy? Can devices sense and smell their environment? Can AI really become self-aware and think for itself?

AI can make lives easier. But it also poses a threat to humanity. History shows that there are inevitably unintended consequences when humans blaze new trails. The on-going development of AI, therefore, needs supervision and oversight, which is why I commend Professor Hawking *et al.* for calling for controls.

Beyond that, I don't lay awake at night worrying about rogue machines taking over the planet. I'm not hunkering down for the robot apocalypse as I believe it is far-fetched. If I'm wrong and AI does turn on us, my grandchildren may live to see humanity's final invention.

Posting Date: 20 April 2015

apps explosion

It's been hailed as the greatest shift in technology since the advent of the Internet. We've become obsessed with mobile application software. Also known as "apps", they are the bite-size software programs that people load onto their smart phones and tablet computers.

In 2007, virtually no mobile apps existed. Today, mobile users have literally millions of apps from which to choose. According to technology research firm, Gartner, more than 102 billion apps were downloaded in 2013. This figure is expected to rise to a mind-boggling 268 billion downloads in 2017.

The mobile app industry is dominated by two giants - Apple's App Store and Google's Play Store. Apple launched its app store in July 2008 to distribute free and paid-for applications for iPhones. Three months later, Google followed suit with its play store for Android-based phones.

Apple and Google each have over 1.2 billion apps available on their respective platforms for download. The most popular apps category is games. This is followed by business, education and lifestyle. A game called *Candy Crush* is the most liked apps game on the planet.

Apps increase the scope of what a mobile device can do and enables users to bank, shop and do almost anything online. People use apps to deliver news, book flights, arrange accommodation, split bills, order meals, play music and navigate cities.

Technology buffs use apps to virtually run their lives. From the moment they wake up (to an app, of course), it's a case of "life on demand" with technology embedded in every aspect of their day. They use apps to get the weather forecast, locate their nearest coffee shop and take their pulse.

With millions of apps at your fingertips, you can find one to satisfy almost any need. Let's say you wanted to visit Sydney "virtually". You can download an app that will let you "explore" the Sydney Opera House and another that will show you the surf conditions at famous Bondi Beach.

To quote one clever headline writer, we've become "the planet of the apps". But there are early signs that app fatigue may be setting in with consumers becoming more selective about what apps they download. Notwithstanding this, consumers are spending more time using their favourite apps.

Mobile apps are popular because mobile search is currently poor and apps layout content in a small-screen, friendly way. However, there is only so much storage space on a smart phone and downloading individual apps and opening them for separate services is predicted to become a thing of the past.

In the future, according to one report, apps will serve as notification systems that push content out as necessary - not big bulky icons that take up prime homepage real estate on our smart phones. This will become increasingly important as screen sizes decrease to that of a smart watch.

In the words of one expert:

> The current web is "pull-based", meaning we visit websites or download mobile applications. The future of the web is "push-based", meaning the web will be coming to us. In the next 10 years, we will witness a transformation from a pull-based web to a push-based web.

Regardless as to whether we find content (pull down) or it finds us (push out), mobile apps will play an increasing role in our lives. Take banking as an example. In many parts of the world, more people now use mobile devices to do their banking than desktop computers.

The mobile-only customer is on the rise and businesses need to adjust accordingly. To this end, Google recently changed the way it ranks searches. It now prioritises companies with "mobile-friendly" websites when people use the search engine on their smart phones or tablet computers.

These mobile devices, replete with apps, may be small but they are having a big impact on society. According to *Forbes* magazine, this year the app economy is expected to reach $100 billion. It's clear that the mobile society has become pervasive - and it's here to stay.

Posting Date: 1 June 2015

banking revolution

Banking is ripe for disruption from the digital revolution sweeping through the financial services sector. The old branch model of retail banking is giving way to mobile and Internet banking. And thanks to a new breed of technology entrepreneurs, the staid world of banking faces an even greater shake up.

Traditional banks and other long established players are being challenged by start-ups that are using technology to find new ways to solve old problems. These "FinTech" companies are giving customers greater control over how they spend, move and manage their money.

The term FinTech is a contraction of the words "financial" and "technology". It has become a ubiquitous term for any technology applied to conducting financial services activities. FinTech has spawned a whole new industry which is reinventing business models using customer centric design.

In December 2014, KPMG released a report listing the top 50 FinTech innovators in the world that are "using technology to the best advantage and driving disruption within the financial services industry". That list includes the four Australian companies shown below.

- *SocietyOne* is a peer-to-peer loan platform enabling individuals to borrow money and lend to each other without the intermediation of a bank.

- *Nimble* is an online credit provider offering short term loans for periods of 16-50 days for amounts from $100 to $1200.

- *Stockpot* is a paperless, online asset allocation tool

enabling users to build an investment portfolio and seek advice online.

- *Metamako* is a high frequency trading hardware maker for financial markets.

Other Australian FinTech companies include personal financial manager, *Pocketbook*, online retail foreign exchange broker, *OzForex*, and independent eftpos provider, *Tyro Payments*. Beyond our shores, payments innovator, *Square*, and crowdfunder, *Kickstarter*, are offering disruptive alternatives to services traditionally provided by banks.

FinTech companies are also helping people manage their entire financial lives with online tools. These tools are at the core of personal financial management (PFM) software such as those offered by *Yodlee* and *Mint.com*. PFM solutions pull together all of a customer's financial information from multiple accounts.

Using PFM, you can track all your financial accounts in one place - savings, credit cards, investments - and easily generate budgets and forecasts to better manage your finances. These online aggregation services are another example of FinTech providers undermining the traditional value proposition of banks.

Last April, Deloitte released a report titled, *Digital disruption: Threats and opportunities for retail financial services*. In that report, Deloitte warns that the finance industry faces an unprecedented series of threats from a new breed of hyper competitive players that are challenging conventions:

> What if payments could be made without using banks as intermediary, and faster? What if money could be borrowed from institutions other than a bank, at a lower rate? What if providers were perceived as directly helping consumers achieve their ultimate goal

(after all, no-one wishes to get a mortgage but rather, dreams of buying a house)?

Deloitte notes that "these new, agile and hitherto largely unregulated players are emerging and are disintermediating the traditional incumbents. Deloitte goes on to say that "regulation is making it harder to innovate and to grow... preventing existing players from responding aggressively to these threats".

It has never been easier, cheaper or faster to create a new business. The Internet allows agile entrepreneurs to capitalise on new opportunities more effectively than large incumbents. Little wonder that FinTech is one of the fastest growing sectors in the financial services industry globally.

There is now talk about the "de-banked" consumer who doesn't need a bank. An example of this is a new payment service by *Snapchat*, the online messaging service. It has teamed up with payments provider, *Square*, to create Snapcash. This enables a Snapchat member to pay another member by sending a message with a dollar amount, totally bypassing banks.

Financial institutions are not alone in battling disruption. Hotels are battling *Airbnb*, taxis are battling *Uber* and publishers are battling *iBooks*. Technology will continue to shape business models over the next decade. It's a case of adapt or perish as only the fittest will survive.

Posting Date: 23 February 2015

driverless cars

They are just around the corner and will appear on a road near you in the not too distant future. Audi has announced that its driverless A8 luxury limousine will be released in 2017. Nissan has declared that it will release a self-drive car by 2018. And Ford says its fully autonomous vehicles will be on the market by 2020.

Most major auto brands plus tech giant, Google, are in the race to put a robot chauffeur in our vehicles. In the coming years, sitting in the driver's seat of a car exclaiming: "Look, no hands!" will not be a joke but a reality. Google has released a prototype of a self-driving car which has no steering wheel, accelerator or brake pedal.

Proponents of fully autonomous vehicles assert that they will eliminate human error which is the cause of most accidents. Humans are emotional creatures who can and do make rash decisions when behind the wheel. As fallible drivers we speed, cut corners, run red lights, stray into the wrong lane and get frustrated in heavy traffic.

Driverless cars, on the other hand, are void of these human foibles and operate on logic. The computer-driven "horseless carriages" of the future will be programmed to behave cautiously and obey instructions. A car's control system will not get tired, drunk or impatient. It will always signal when turning and won't put the pedal to the metal, talk on the phone or succumb to road rage.

It is claimed that driverless cars could dominate roads in the next 15 years. Driverless technology uses a range of devices - including cameras, sensors, radars, GPS and computer vision - to constantly monitor a vehicle's surroundings. These control systems interpret sensory information to identify appropriate navigation paths as well as obstacles.

Another claim is that driverless vehicles will "talk" to each other using vehicle-to-vehicle (V2V) communication technology. This should provide motorists with not only a quicker journey but a safer one - V2V can activate an emergency stop to prevent a collision.

These purported benefits make state-of-the-art, self-drive vehicles sound like auto utopia. But is this really the case? Driverless cars will free us to work, rest, play and chat while in transit, so commute time will no longer be down time. However, I'm not ready to get in my car, go to sleep and wake up at my destination as if being transported like cargo.

I actually like driving and being in control of my vehicle. Also, I'm not convinced that all the computer bugs have been ironed out yet. What happens if glaring sun blinds a car's cameras? How will a driverless car react to road rage from another vehicle? What about insurance? Who pays if your robot-driven car causes an accident?

Test trials of driverless vehicles have shown that the technology's record is not squeaky clean. Google's test fleet of autonomous cars has been involved in 11 accidents. Nonetheless, I have no doubt that the technology will get better and that sooner rather than later driverless cars will get the green light from traffic authorities. But I won't be an early adopter of robotic cars.

In 1942, science fiction writer, Isaac Asimov, suggested "rules" to govern the behaviour of robots. These three rules have since become known as Asimov's Laws and state:

- A robot may not injure a human being or, through inaction, allow a human being to come to harm.

- A robot must obey the orders given it by human beings, except where such orders would conflict with the First Law.

- A robot must protect its own existence as long as such protection does not conflict with the First or Second Laws.

While Asimov tried to give machines a moral code, this is not possible in reality. This begs the question: What will a driverless car do when faced with a moral dilemma? Ethicists say that you face a moral dilemma when you are required to do each of two actions but can only do one of the actions. Let me illustrate this dilemma with an example.

A driverless car has an obligation to keep its passengers safe. It also has an obligation to do no harm to pedestrians. But what if those two obligations clash? Let's say a runaway truck is careering out of control and will crash head-on into a driverless vehicle. The vehicle's computer has a duty of care to protect the passengers and take evasive action.

But in taking the only evasive action available, the robot driver must mount the footpath (sidewalk) where a group of primary school children is standing. I can't say with certainty what a mechanical driver would do in this situation, but I know what I would do as a human driver.

The bottom line is that life is not always black and white. Sometimes the line between right and wrong is blurred. We humans rely on nuanced readings of complex situations while machines have no such subtlety. That's why the human brain is considered the most sophisticated machine in the universe. At this stage, I'd rather put my life in my own hands than that of a machine.

Posting Date: 31 August 2015

wearable technology

It's the year 2020. You have just woken from your slumber and are getting dressed to leave home for the day. Wearable technology is now an integral part of your everyday life and you put on a slew of devices. Your walking shoes contain a GPS navigation system, your sports shirt tracks the amount of calories you burn while your wrist band monitors your heart rate.

Welcome to the brave new world of smart clothes and smart watches. Wearables are trumpeted as the perfect marriage between technology and fashion. If the futurists are right, many of us will soon be wearing circuits, sensors and batteries on our bodies. Smart garments that integrate phones and cameras will also be commonplace.

Imagine a bride walking down the aisle with a camera woven into her wedding veil to capture her special day. Or a guest at the same wedding wearing a smart jacket with a twitter feed so that he can tweet about the big day. Not to be forgotten is the chief bridesmaid who wears a hat with built-in mood adjusting headphones to get her through a stressful day.

Sound far-fetched? Well, what about smart fingernails which display holographic designs that are scanned using a phone app? How about a Bluetooth dress that lights up for incoming calls? There's even a bra designed to shock attackers and then send a text message to a relative or friend and the local police with the GPS coordinates of the victim's location.

Wearable technology has even made its way to the staid world of banking. A Canadian bank is trialling a heartbeat monitoring wristband to authenticate contactless payments. In Australia, a regional bank has developed a merino wool "power suit" with an embedded contactless chip and antenna fused into the sleeve. The wearer pays by passing his cuff over a payment terminal.

It can be seen that wearables have myriad applications. But will they go from high-tech novelty to everyday necessity? Put another way, will they transition from geek fad to mega trend? As always, this is the $64 million question. Some believe that wearables are a solution in search of a problem. Others see wearables as the way to seamlessly integrate technology into our lives.

Research reveals that people want their technology to not only solve a problem, but to look attractive. This is one of the reasons why Google Glass failed - it looked like a geeky gadget in lieu of a chic fashion accessory. Fashion, of course, is a very personal thing, so designers of wearables need to be savvy and offer consumers choice.

It's clear that the tech world has a lot to learn about fashion. It's not just a case of "if you build it they will come". Aesthetics play an important role in fashion and the current range of wearables falls far short of being glamorous. Tech companies have to get much better at merging function with form to put "wear" into wearables and make smart-tech sexy.

To date, the bigger fashion houses in Europe have shown a general disdain for wearables. In contrast, well known clothing brand, Ralph Lauren, is an enthusiastic early adopter. The company's iconic polo shirts have gone high tech. The PoloTech Shirt uses biometric sensors to collect real-time workout data from the wearer's movement.

One of the issues with wearables is privacy. If I am wired for connectivity, my whereabouts can always be tracked. That might be of benefit if you are someone who frequently gets lost. Beyond that, I don't want my every move monitored. This is already happening - some companies have introduced wearables to measure how active their employees have been.

Regular readers of this blog will not be surprised to learn

that I won't be rushing out to buy wearable technology. I am a true Doubting Thomas when it comes to the unmitigated hype and gushing praise surrounding new technology. Despite being heralded as game-changers, Google Glass did not live up to expectations nor has the Apple Watch set the world on fire.

With regard to technology, I am on the record as saying that robots will not take over the planet and that Bitcoins will not replace fiat currencies. Let me again stick my neck out and say that I cannot see wearable technology becoming the new dress code for the masses any time soon. I, for one, don't want to be connected to the Internet 24 hours a day.

Posting Date: 21 September 2015

megatall buildings

It has been described as the adult equivalent of little boys peeing against a wall. The race by world renowned architects to build the tallest tower on the planet is not without its critics. But erecting an iconic, gravity-defying building that soars to the heavens gives a city enormous bragging rights.

Currently, the granddaddy of them all is Dubai's Burj Khalifa building which stands at 828 metres - more than twice the height of the Empire State Building. The Burj dwarfs all other buildings around it and boasts the world's longest elevator ride and the world's highest outdoor observation deck.

But the Burj will lose the mantle of world's tallest man-made structure in 2019 when it is usurped by the Kingdom Tower in Jeddah, Saudi Arabia. The gargantuan Kingdom Tower will be the first building ever to exceed the lofty height of 1,000 metres or 1 km. (The exact height is being kept a secret.)

This begs the question: How far can we go in building these "vertical cities"? Well, believe it or not, American architect, Adrian Smith, has designed a scale model of a mile-high (1.6 km) skyscraper. This is twice the height of the Burj or four Empire State Buildings stacked on top of one another.

Smith and his team designed both the Burj Khalifa and the Kingdom Tower and believe a mile-high building is feasible. They just need to find someone prepared to pay the billion-dollar-plus price tag to construct such a jaw-dropping skyscraper that will push the limits of design.

The world was in awe in 1931 when the 381 metre Empire State Building was completed. It held the title of the world's tallest building until 1972 when it was passed by the 417 metre World Trade Centre in New York. Then the grip on the title of world's tallest building became more tenuous.

TECHNOLOGICAL ADVANCES

This started with the completion of the 442 metre Sears Tower in Chicago in 1974 followed by the 452 metre Petronas Towers in Kuala Lumpur in 1998. Next was the 509 metre Taipai 101 Tower in 2003 and finally the 828 metre Burj Khalifa in 2010.

According to the Council on Tall Buildings & Urban Habitat, a building is defined as "supertall" if it is over 300 metres in height and "megatall" if it reaches over 600 metres. As at June 2015, there were 91 supertall and two megatall buildings* fully completed and occupied globally.

The world is in the midst of a skyscraper boom with 19 of the 20 tallest buildings constructed in the past 20 years. Asia and the Middle East are leading the high rise boom. The once mighty Empire State Building has been relegated to the 28th rung on the ladder of world's tallest buildings.

[Please allow me to insert a parenthetical note here. I have visited the Empire State Building and many other famous skyscrapers. I must be a big kid as I enjoy the view from high-rise observation decks. Among the buildings I have visited include the Sears Tower (now called the Willis Tower), The Petronas Towers and the Burj Khalifa. Next stop Jeddah?]

Advancements in design and construction have enabled the creation of buildings that would have been unimaginable a few decades ago. In reaching new heights, skyscrapers present unique and formidable challenges to architects and engineers, with a major technical challenge being the wind.

Supertall and megatall buildings face greater wind pressures as wind speeds at high altitude are much greater than at ground level. Architects, therefore, need to design aerodynamic buildings to deal structurally with wind loading. Models of building designs are tested in wind tunnels to ensure they can withstand the extreme winds to which they will be subjected.

Another technical challenge is "vertical transportation". Put simply, this refers to lift technology - how to move people up and down the building. The steel cables used to suspend lifts are subjected to huge strain. This is mostly due to the weight of the actual cable itself, which can well exceed the weight of the elevator and its passengers.

Finnish elevator company, Kone, has solved this problem with the development of a new carbon fibre cable called UltraRope. Strong and lightweight, UltraRope will allow lifts to travel up to 1km in a single run - double what's currently possible with a steel cable.

Theoretically, there is no ceiling on how tall a building can be. If developers keep thinking tall and architects keep pushing the envelope, the sky may well be the limit for megatall buildings. Clearly, the race to the top is not over yet.

[*NOTE: The second megatall building is the 601m Royal Clock Tower Hotel in Mecca. This building never held the title of world's tallest building as it was completed in 2012 i.e., two years after the Burj.]

Posting Date: 14 September 2015

bad predictions

In 1962, British rock band, The Beatles, were told that "guitar music is on the way out". In 1996, Harry Potter author, J.K. Rowling, was told that "children just aren't interested in witches and wizards anymore". In 2007, Apple founder, Steve Jobs, was told that "there's no chance that the iPhone is going to get any significant market share".

Clearly, prophecy is a tricky business, but that hasn't stopped hordes of people from trying to forecast the future. There are myriad examples of famous last words including "radio has no future", "television is a flash in the pan", "a rocket will never be able to leave the Earth's atmosphere" and "the Internet will catastrophically collapse".

As I pointed out in a previous post, *The certainty of uncertainty*, crystal ball gazers rarely get it right. While people want to know what will happen in the future, the truth is that no one really knows. But that has not stopped "experts" in a range of fields making fools of themselves by offering predictions that turn out to be hopelessly wrong.

Around the time I started my working life, futurists were saying that by the 21st century, technology would have reduced the need for labour. The concern back then was that automation would usher in a fifteen hour working week and we would all be bored with an over-abundance of leisure time. I think it's fair to say that prediction was a bit wide of the mark! Today, most of us are time poor with working parents particularly feeling the pressure.

Another inaccurate forecast was the demise of shopping centres. Internet shopping, we were told, would spell the end of bricks-and-mortar retailing. While online commerce has taken off, it has not made the high street store extinct. Indeed, shopping centres remain magnets around Christmas and other peak shopping periods. People still flock to the shops despite the queues and lack of parking.

Movie theatres were also put on the endangered species list following the release of home videos. But the long predicted drama - "Death of the Cinema!" - has not eventuated. Cinemas are thriving with the advent of multiplexes and luxury cinemas. Today, moviegoers can experience plush seats with call buttons, oversized screens with surround sound and exclusive lounges with complimentary refreshments.

One prediction that may not be fantasy relates to booksellers. The collapse of many bookselling chains suggests we may be nearing the end for embattled bookstores. Store footprints have definitely shrunk, but those that remain are re-writing their business plans to stay relevant. As a book-lover, I remain hopeful that bookstores will be able to shake off their dust jackets and start a new chapter.

To end this little history lesson on failed prognostications, I thought I'd turn to a sector I know well - financial services. As with other areas of the business world, banking has had its fair share of false prophets. Economists predicted things which never came to pass like the nationalisation of all banks, the collapse of money and the death of the Euro.

On the other hand, something that did happen but was not forecast by economists was the Global Financial Crisis (GFC). The GFC was the most destructive financial shock since the Great Depression and it brought the free market to the precipice. As I wrote in a 2009 blog post, *Credit crisis a mid-life crisis for economists*, economists failed to spot the GFC and this put the profession under the spotlight.

As one commentator noted at the time: "An entire field of experts dedicated to studying the behaviour of markets failed to anticipate what may prove to be the biggest economic collapse of our lifetime." The GFC was a humbling experience for economic forecasters and left people wondering whether economists really know any more than the rest of us. This justifiable scepticism applies to all self-proclaimed soothsayers.

The harsh reality is that the world is too complex to accurately predict what will happen down the track. As technology accelerates this complexity, it's becoming less predictable. So, ignore those who claim to know the future. Behind their bravado, they invariably know little more than the rest of us. The simple truth is that humans are inherently bad at predicting the future.

Posting Date: 9 March 2015

space economy

You may not have noticed, but there is a battle going on at the moment. It's between three billionaires who are all trying to conquer the next frontier. Renowned businessman, Richard Branson, Amazon founder, Jeff Bezos and PayPal co-founder, Elon Musk, are in a race to take well-heeled passengers to space.

These billionaire "astropreneurs" are looking beyond Earth and investing in commercial space flights. They hope to usher in a new era of space travel and exploration. While each tycoon is pursuing different goals, they are united in their desire to reach for the stars in seeking out extra-terrestrial business opportunities which provide out-of-this-world experiences.

The first mover in the mogul's space race was Jeff Bezos who established the private space flight firm, Blue Origin, in 2000. Next off the launch pad was Elon Musk who in 2002 set up space exploration firm, SpaceX. Finally, Richard Branson joined the billionaire's space club in 2004 with the founding of space tourism firm, Virgin Galactic.

Branson's goal is to make short trips to suborbital space for those wishing to experience weightlessness and glimpse the Earth. Bezos is more adventurous and wants to launch astronauts to both suborbital and orbital space. Meanwhile, Musk is by far the most ambitious with a vision "to make life multi-planetary" by sending humans to Mars.

Over the longer term, Branson believes his spacecraft can be modified into supersonic jets that will make suborbital, intercontinental travel possible. These Concorde-like aircraft will travel outside of the Earth's atmosphere at incredibly fast speeds. Using gravitational forces, suborbital jets could cut the journey time from Sydney to London to just over two hours.

Rocket man, Jeff Bezos, has a loftier goal for humanity. He wants to see "millions of people living and working in space". He believes that humans are "...really evolved to be pioneers" and that "new worlds have a way of saving old worlds". He is confident that his interstellar ambition will take off and that leaving the Earth's atmosphere will ultimately become accessible to many.

For outer-space pioneer, Elon Musk, the quest is about much more than space jaunts. He wants to routinely launch crews to the International Space Station. With the shuttle era over, Musk intends to build rockets for NASA like Boeing builds airplanes for airlines. He also wants to establish a permanent, self-sustaining colony on Mars.

Branson, Bezos and Musk are not the only rocket-ship revolutionaries. Investing in commercial space flight has become popular among the ultra-wealthy. The heavens are getting crowded with billionaires who want to reshape space flight. The band of rich rocketeers is growing with new space buffs recently joining the nascent space industry.

Google co-founder, Larry Page, and Google Chairman, Eric Schmidt, are among several billionaire investors backing Planetary Resources Inc., a company founded in 2012 to mine asteroids. Asteroids are rich in untapped resources ranging from precious metals to water. The Google duo believes that mining asteroids will "add trillions of dollars to the global GDP" and "help ensure humanity's prosperity".

Another billionaire with galactic ambitions is Microsoft co-founder, Paul Allen. Earlier this year he established Vulcan Aerospace. Allen wants "to shift how the world conceptualizes space travel through cost reduction and on-demand access". He believes that "the drive toward new frontiers is integral to our humanity".

It seems that the world is not enough for Earth's titans of

business who want to be masters of the universe. From cyber-space to outer-space, their reach is rocketing upward. Personally, I think we are entering a very exciting era of human discovery. I'm sure my grandkids will enjoy their zero gravity rides.

Beam me up, Scotty!

Posting Date: 9 November 2015

tomorrow's jobs

Here's a headline-grabbing figure: 65% of today's primary school children will work in jobs that do not currently exist, according to a US Department of Labor report. The careers of Generation Z will be far more focussed on technology than that of the current workforce, a trend that is already evident.

Many of today's hottest jobs - apps developer, data miner, cloud technologist, social-media manager and user-experience designer - were unheard of a decade or so ago. Looking ahead, we will likely see demand for digital architects, avatar designers, 3D printing engineers, content curators and cyber-security officers.

How do you prepare today's students for these jobs of tomorrow? In short, you need to give education systems a digital-age upgrade. I believe that students still need to be taught the three Rs - Reading, wRiting and aRithmetic. Additionally, children must also learn programming and coding as part of the core curriculum to ensure that they are digitally literate for their future workplaces.

It is a real challenge to prepare students for jobs that have not been created, technologies that have not been invented and problems that have not yet arisen. But this is the education imperative in the 21st century where new industries and occupations will continue to emerge and old industries and jobs will decline.

No one really knows whether automation will create as many jobs as it renders obsolete. What is clear is that preparing students for jobs of the past is a recipe for disaster. It is imperative that kids become learners for life and have the ability to embrace and adapt to rapid changes in a world where people will increasingly live and work online.

In the future, it may well be commonplace to walk into a

restaurant and order your meal using a tablet computer. Similarly, you may be able to have your online shopping delivered to your home in a self-driving truck. If these scenarios become reality, what does the future hold for waiters and truck drivers? Will low skilled workers be more quickly displaced than others?

Jobs growth is predicted in aged care, the environment and technology. Not every high school or university graduate, therefore, needs to be a technology geek. But given the predicted rise in "knowledge workers", today's students need to be taught skills in problem solving, teamwork, creativity and innovative thinking.

Recently, the Foundation for Young Australians (FYA) released a report warning that young people will be the hardest hit under a new future of work. The report states that "…60% of Australian students are currently studying or training for occupations where at least two-thirds of jobs will be automated over the coming decades".

It goes on to say that "…we need to provide our young people with a different set of skills - to allow them to navigate their way through a diverse employment journey that will include around five career changes and an average of 17 different jobs". The FYA believes our national curriculum is stuck in the past with teaching in digital skills not commencing until Year 9 despite international evidence that it should start earlier.

It is clear that our information based economy is craving more intellectual property which requires a new kind of learning environment. The challenge facing educators is to develop curriculum which equips students with the knowledge and skills required to lead successful and fulfilling lives in the 21st century.

When I started school in 1962, I sat at a desk with an inkwell and listened to a teacher whose main pedagogical aids were a stick of chalk and a blackboard. Classrooms were designed for lecture and crowd control, with the teacher as the central figure of knowledge and authority. Students took notes in lesson books which were used for later revision.

The classrooms of tomorrow will be high-tech environments configured around student-centred learning hubs. They will feature 3D printers, tablet computers and even robotic teachers. Students will have digital tools such as laptops and smartphones. Subject matter experts will deliver lectures via holographic images while interactive videos will help students with homework.

We are on the cusp of a brave new world of learning!

Posting Date: 30 November 2015

networkedsociety

Technological development is occurring at an exponential rate. We are being swept up in a global information revolution which shows no signs of abating. As each year passes we witness rapid changes in the way we communicate, learn, work and play. The common thread is our need to be connected.

Mobile phones have become ubiquitous, going from "yuppie-toy" to "must-have" in a relatively short period of time. Today, more humans own a mobile phone than do not. Mobiles have become the most common consumer electronics devices on Earth.

Text messaging has enhanced the utility of mobiles since the first text message was sent in 1992. There are now more text messages sent and received every day than the number of people on the planet. It's estimated that over 200,000 text messages are sent every second.

In addition to phoning and texting, we also like to e-mail. During 2010, an estimated 294 billion e-mails were sent every day among the world's 1.4 billion e-mail users. The average office worker is estimated to spend around 40% of their working day sending and receiving e-mails.

We also like to keep in contact via Facebook. Facebook's user population exceeds a staggering 500 million people. If Facebook were a country, it would occupy the third position after China and India in terms of population. One-third of Australians are Facebook members.

But wait - there's more! We love to Google the cyber universe. In 2006, Google received 2.7 billion search requests every month. Today, that figure is 31 billion and climbing. Facebook is Australia's number one Google search request.

Technology is clearly fulfilling a basic human need for togetherness and belonging. Perhaps that explains the phenomenal growth in online dating with singles looking for love over the Internet. One in eight couples in the US who married in 2007 met via social media.

Every part of our daily lives, from transactional banking to grocery shopping, is affected by technology. Some find it hard to remember how things were in the "good old days". The world we see today would not be recognisable to people of a few generations ago.

My grandfather thought it was amazing that a remote control - wired to the TV set with a 20 foot long cable - could change the channels on his black & white television. Given the way technology is heading, my grandchildren may have a remote device to control their entire life - both real and virtual!

Posting Date: 21 March 2011

cloudcomputing

If you believe the IT industry, there's a seismic shift going on at the moment. It's undetectable to the masses, but computer geeks know it's real. It's poised to radically alter the way we access information technology and it's called cloud computing.

The word "cloud" is a metaphor for the Internet and cloud computing refers to Internet based computing. It enables you to "rent" software instead of buying it and means your computing resources reside outside of your computer or physical premises.

With cloud computing others take care of your computing needs. You no longer need to purchase applications, back up disks, upgrade software or maintain security. You simply run your applications in the cloud and access them via the web. All of your data and files are stored in the cloud.

Cloud computing - outsourcing hardware and software to Internet service providers - is an example of "disruptive technology". Such technology is ground breaking, dislocates the normal flow, creates a true paradigm shift and replaces the market leader.

Electricity is an example of disruptive technology and cloud computing is set to join its ranks in revolutionising our lives. Just as we plug-in to the ubiquitous electricity outlet to get our electricity, we are increasingly plugging-in to the Internet's global computing grid to power our IT needs.

"Computing is turning into a utility," writes Nicholas Carr in *The Big Switch: Rewiring The World, From Edison To Google*. A hundred years ago companies stopped generating their own power and plugged into the newly built electric grid. "Today," says Carr, "we're in the midst of another epochal transformation, and it's following a similar course."

"In the years ahead," argues Carr, "more and more of the information-processing tasks that we rely on, at home and at work, will be handled by big data centres located out on the Internet." These data centres are referred to as server farms and Google has built the world's largest facility in Oregon. Locally, Telstra has just announced its intention to offer cloud computing services. And Westpac Bank has built its own private cloud computing facility.

Web-based e-mail services like Hotmail, Yahoo! and Gmail are examples of cloud computing. Users log into a remote, e-mail account. The software and storage for the account doesn't exist on the user's computer but resides on the e-mail provider's computer cloud.

Social networking sites, like Facebook, are another example of cloud services. The cloud also hosts a free web-based personal financial management service called Mint.

It's predicted that by 2020, most consumers will access software applications through the use of remote server networks. With claims that server farms can carry out a computer task for one-tenth of the cost incurred by the average IT department, I have no doubt that the corporate world will increasingly jump on the cloud bandwagon.

Posting Date: 18 October 2010

business models

With the advent of the Internet, a growing number of firms have abandoned conventional ways of doing business. They have adopted a new business model called "the platform". The early adopters of the platform model - Amazon, Apple, Facebook and Google - have redefined how business is done and how value is created.

By way of background, a business model provides the basic template for how a business will compete in the marketplace. It defines what a business does and how it makes money doing those things. Put simply, a business model is the operating framework used by a company to generate revenue and make a profit from its operations.

More formally, a business model reveals the way a firm converts inputs (raw materials, labour) into outputs (goods and services) to deliver a return to investors. Since the Industrial Revolution, companies have used this linear business model to create value, which is pushed out to consumers as an end product. Under the linear model, value flows in one direction.

In contrast, companies today are increasingly using technology to transform their traditional linear business models into networked, platform models. A platform business model connects two or more third parties and allows them to interact with each other. The fundamental goal of the platform model is to facilitate collaboration.

The linear model represents a standalone way of doing business whereas platforms require companies to be team players. TV channels work on a linear model while YouTube is a platform model. The once mighty Encyclopedia Britannica utilises a linear model and has been overshadowed by Wikipedia which builds value using a platform model.

A recent Harvard Business Review article offered this explanation:

> In construction, a platform is something that lifts you up and on which others can stand. The same is true in business. By building a digital platform, other businesses can easily connect their business with yours, build products and services on top of it, and co-create value. This ability to "plug-and-play" is a defining characteristic of platform thinking.
>
> Consider the market for smartphones. Nokia and Blackberry today are a shadow of their former glory. Their technology and products lag Apple and the Android ecosystem. But the triumph of Apple and Android is not from features and functions. It is from the app store on which external developers create value.

Using terminology coined by digital consultants, platform companies are referred to as "Network Orchestrators". These companies create a network of peers in which the participants interact and share in the value creation. They may sell products or services, build relationships, share advice, give reviews, collaborate and co-create. Examples include Airbnb, Uber and eBay.

Airbnb does not own a single hotel room, Uber does not own a fleet of taxi cabs and eBay does not operate retail outlets. But these peer-to-peer businesses allow anyone to become a hotelier, a taxi driver or a retailer. It's called collaborative consumption and it's made possible via the sharing economy which is underpinned by the platform business model.

With businesses like Wikipedia, YouTube and Facebook, the user does all the work. Users write content, upload videos and share life experiences. As a result of this collaboration, Wikipedia has become the world's largest repository of knowledge, YouTube is the world's biggest video content library and Facebook is the world's greatest warehouse of personal information.

Unlike linear models, platforms do more than just manufacture and push things out - they allow consumers to create and share value. Facilitating interactions between multiple parties creates rapid scalability. With a market capitalization of US$700 billion, Apple is the planet's most valuable company, not because it makes great devices, but because it has the best platform.

Some believe that peer-to-peer lending platforms are set to transform the consumer lending industry. These platforms don't lend their own funds but match borrowers directly with investors - so there's no need for a bank in the middle. Like other platform businesses, everything is done online with loans approved within a few hours.

It's clear that digital platform business models are disrupting every industry and rapidly making the traditional linear business model obsolete. The new models are winning the hearts and minds of consumers with their customer-centric focus. In banking, as in other industries, the future belongs to those with business models that put the customer centre stage.

Posting Date: 1 February 2016

energy challenges

The world's appetite for electricity is projected to more than double between 2008 and 2035. The energy-hungry nations of China and India are fuelling much of this growth. Moreover, the Internet's energy footprint, generated by over 1.5 billion online users, is growing at a rate of 10% per annum.

The supply of electricity is not keeping pace with demand. Many parts of the world live with daily rolling blackouts. More electricity needs to be produced but it can't be pumped directly out of the ground like oil or captured from moving air like wind.

Electricity is a secondary energy source - it's obtained from the conversion of primary energy sources such as coal, gas, oil, solar power, hydro power and nuclear energy. These energy sources can be classified as either renewable or non-renewable, but electricity itself is neither renewable nor non-renewable.

Australia has an abundant supply of renewable energy resources including solar, wind and water. Yet we rely on non-renewable energy (fossil fuels) for 95% of our energy needs. Of this, coal provides 40%, oil 33% and gas 22%.

Following the Copenhagen Climate Change Summit, many nations - including Australia - pledged to reduce carbon emissions. Coal accounts for about 37% of Australia's greenhouse gas emissions which is why the Australian government wants a tax on carbon emissions from "dirty" coal-fired generators.

Presently, coal-fired power is cheaper than using non-polluting energy supplies such as nuclear power. Energy producers, therefore, are unlikely to voluntarily choose environmentally friendly forms of energy as they are more expensive and less efficient compared to coal-fired electricity.

Ergo, the government's decision to force a mandatory change in the mix of energy production via a carbon tax to facilitate effective greenhouse gas mitigation. Westpac Bank is supporting the government's efforts and will not finance any new high carbon emitting assets. Westpac will focus on the development of clean energy solutions.

Over the past year, electricity prices in Australia have risen by more than 20%. A carbon tax will push up prices further. Higher prices, it is argued, will cause consumers to modify their demand and become more responsible users of electricity. But is this really the case?

The tax on alcopops increased the price of pre-mixed alcoholic beverages but didn't dampen demand among teenagers. So, do we really believe that demand for electricity, which is predicted to more than double by 2050 in Australia, will fall due to a carbon tax?

I can't see "plugged-in" Australian households turning off their air conditioners or buying less power-hungry TVs due to higher electricity prices. My sense is that electricity consumption per capita will continue to increase. A prosperous society like Australia uses many modern, energy-consuming appliances.

My advice - unless you are one of those rare and precious individuals who is truly into energy efficiency - is to budget for higher power bills. Supplying power to the people is a costly exercise. As long as we continue to flick the switch, we'll continue to pay the price.

Posting Date: 24 January 2011

05
Christmas Parodies

▪▪ Chapter Overview

This final chapter contains eight parodies of the classic poem, *The Night Before Christmas.* It is a corporate tradition at Gateway Credit Union that the last blog post published at the end of the calendar year takes a light-hearted look at the year that was. The annual year-in-review is set to the rhythm and rhyme scheme of Clement Moore's original lyric while addressing a different subject matter - Australia's and the world's economic and social performance during the preceding twelve months. Note that the final stanza in each parody is identical. It is hoped that the reader does not find this repetition wearisome.

christmas 2008

'Twas the week before Christmas and Gateway was well,
The staff were excited, it wasn't hard to tell.
St Nick is coming, there's little time to spare,
A flurry of activity fills the credit union air.

I'm busy blogging with mouse and worn keyboard,
I try to ensure each blog strikes an interesting chord.
One last message before the year comes to a close,
But keep it simple and don't overdo the prose.

I reflect on a year that was filled with gloom,
And wonder why we humans focus on doom.
The year will go down as our *annus horribilis,*
Our wealth tumbled far and this did not thrill us.

The credit crisis was challenging, we
all looked for an answer,
But for now our thoughts focus on Dancer and Prancer.
We'll let the year pass, because another is coming,
Let's hope a new dawn sees the economy humming.

Now Gary, now Loyce, now Peter and Paul,
You've worked hard all year, so dash away all.
Don't dilly, don't dally, move merrily as you now flee,
Go home to families and presents
beneath the sparkling tree.

As I sign off for Christmas I thank each and every member,
It's been a pleasure to serve you, right through to December.
May the joy of the season fill your home on Christmas Day,
As we smile and gently whisper,
"Merry Christmas" from Gateway.

Posting Date: 22 December 2008

christmas 2009

'Twas the week before Christmas,
when all through the nation,
Australians were preparing for a quiet vacation.
It's been a year to remember, but we'd rather forget,
The tales of horror from a calamitous threat.

While brokers sat watching their stocks by night,
Investors moved faster than Rudolph in flight.
They didn't dilly or dally or pause as they sold,
Shares tumbled far, unless they were gold.

Caused by market traders who some now despise,
The global crisis took most by surprise.
But like all sordid tales of excess and greed,
We love blaming others, it fulfils a need.

We've all learnt lessons, experience is the teacher,
Let's hope we're now wiser than a Sunday school preacher.
But don't be surprised if it all happens again,
The next generation's exuberance will be hard to contain.

Now Rudd, now Swan, now Turnbull and Hockey,
You've squabbled all year, fighting harder than Rocky.
When St Nick asks if you've been naughty or nice,
Tell him politicians aren't made of sugar and spice.

Bailouts and bankruptcies, the future looks bad,
But Santa is coming, so don't be too sad.
With tinsel and presents under the tree,
Please enjoy Christmas, even if it's not debt free.

As I sign off for Christmas I thank each and every member,
It's been a pleasure to serve you, right through to December.
May the joy of the season fill your home on Christmas Day,

BITE SIZE ADVICE 2

As we smile and gently whisper, "Merry Christmas" from Gateway.

Posting Date: 21 December 2009

christmas 2010

'Twas the week before Christmas and Gateway was loud,
We've had a big year and the team is proud.
From winning awards to just doing it right,
We've come out of the shadows and into the light.

In a year that started with great expectations,
We've achieved all we said winning many citations.
But our greatest triumph is not measured by fame,
It's sticking to our mantra of staying the same.

We're proud to be a mutual and remain true blue,
Our focus on Members drives all that we do.
Whether it's to borrow, invest or save for a goal,
We're here to help because that's our role.

We took our first steps down the Yellow Brick Road,
And found a strategic partner who lightened our load.
Mark Bouris and his team deserve special mention,
They set the bar high and grabbed lots of attention.

The big banks too were caught in the spotlight,
Their interest rate rises caused a media dogfight.
Banks were vilified, berated and called Uncle Scrooge,
The people lamented, they must think we're a stooge.

Now Julia, now Wayne, now Tony and Joe,
Credit unions and building societies just want a fair go.
As political leaders you've made lots of promises,
It's time to deliver, lest we become Doubting Thomases.

It's been a tough year for all, especially bank bosses,
They received little praise, yet produced no losses.
Each made a contribution in their own special way,
And were handsomely recognised with a multi-million pay.

Interest rates are rising, but the outlook is fair,
Santa is coming, so there's no need to despair.
With tinsel and presents under the tree,
Please enjoy Christmas, even if it's not debt free.

As I sign off for Christmas I thank each and every Member,
It's been a pleasure to serve you, right through to December.
May the joy of the season fill your home on Christmas Day,
As we smile and gently whisper,
"Merry Christmas" from Gateway.

Posting Date: 20 December 2010

christmas 2011

'Twas the week before Christmas and all through the press,
Commentators were opining, Europe's still a mess.
As the year draws to a close, economic problems remain,
So how do we really help Greece, Italy and Spain?

The ancient city of Athens, once a thriving metropolis,
If it gets any worse, they'll have to sell the Acropolis.
It's the season of giving, beware of Greeks bearing a gift,
The lesson is tough, they must learn habits of thrift.

Italy's also in trouble, Berlusconi left in a pickle,
Due to poor fiscal restraint and some slap and tickle.
Dogged by controversy, Italians tolerated
Berlusconi's behaviour,
However he turned out to be, not their
deficit-reduction saviour.

Now a nightmare before Christmas
befalls many a European nation,
As they ponder the possibility of a Eurozone separation.
If the Euro-family stays together, that would be jolly,
But as the squabbling continues,
wishing for peace seems a folly.

Meanwhile Australians rejoice 'cause
our economy's safe and strong,
We're ahead of the pack, by a confident and clear furlong.
While the rest of the world grapples with unsustainable debt,
We're really powering ahead, so there's no need to fret.

A coveted and prestigious title was
bestowed on Wayne Swan,
Voted world's best treasurer for
stewardship deemed spot-on.

Australia dodged a recession and kept the wolves away,
Sound economic management, from
this path we must not stray.

For Gateway the year has been one to remember,
Winning awards and accolades through to December.
We set the bar high, punching above our weight,
Due to determination and teamwork, the results are great.

To the extended Gateway family, the
Yellow Brick Road team,
Thanks for your efforts, which were really supreme.
By working together we've challenged the big banks,
They now know there's competition among their ranks.

Now management, now staff and readers of this blog,
Santa's arrival is imminent, so I will leave you agog.
At this time of year, the child in all of us starts to wonder,
The magic of Christmas, peace and goodwill down-under.

As I sign off for Christmas I thank each and every member,
It's been a pleasure to serve you, right through to December.
May the joy of the season fill your home on Christmas Day,
As we smile and gently whisper "Merry
Christmas" from Gateway.

Posting Date: 19 December 2011

christmas2012

'Twas the week before Christmas in the land Down Under,
The weather forecast was for a season free of thunder.
So, the citizens of this great nation have nothing to fear,
Let's bring on the sun and some good old festive cheer.

Australia's travelling well according to our economic report,
Yet we continue to worry, it's become a national sport.
While the rest of the world struggles with burgeoning debt,
Under the stars of the Southern Cross,
there's no need to fret.

Sure we're not perfect, but we're the envy
of many a developed nation,
In a borderless world, we're a shining
example of globalisation.
We continue to punch above our weight and raise the bar,
International praise is heaped on us,
even though we live afar.

In the sovereign currency beauty parade we wear the crown,
We have the third most traded currency,
which causes some to frown.
The rise and rise of the Aussie dollar is both good and bad,
Consumers are happy while local manufacturers are sad.

Of course, we live in a world of losers and winners,
It's just the way it is, and at the moment we're grinners.
The London Olympics kept the smile on our face,
We're proud of our athletes if not our overall place.

Gateway won gold, being named Credit Union of the Year,
We stood proudly on the winner's dais, full of cheer.
To be recognised as the best is no mean feat,
After being runner-up for years, victory was sweet.

I too felt proud on publishing my 200th blog post,
Forgive me for mentioning it, didn't mean to boast.
They take minutes to read but much longer to prepare,
Hope you enjoyed them, they're crafted with care.

When Santa asks whether I've been naughty or nice,
I'll be quick to respond, he won't have to ask twice.
Both staff and members have been treated fairly,
The responsibility for that rests in my court squarely.

From across the Pacific there will soon be a clatter,
St Nicholas is coming, and he'll be landing at Parramatta.
So, clear your desk and prepare your home,
And don't dilly-dally, put out your garden gnome.

As I sign off for Christmas I thank each and every member,
It's been a pleasure to serve you, right through to December.
May the joy of the season fill your home on Christmas Day,
As we smile and gently whisper "Merry Christmas" from Gateway.

Posting Date: 17 December 2012

christmas 2013

'Tis the week before Christmas and my shopping is done,
But there's something I must complete
before it's time for fun.
Compose a Christmas parody that captures the Yule spirit,
Use poetic licence but stay within the blog word limit.

Where and how to begin is a challenge for sure,
"I've done this before," he says to reassure.
Let the prose begin with rhythm and rhyme,
By the time it's finished you'll hear Christmas chime.

Credit union members were nestled all snug in their beds,
With visions of falling interest rates in their heads.
Borrowers rejoiced, a loan's never been cheaper,
Savers despaired, returns have plummeted steeper.

The debate over rates generated such a clatter,
Yet most agreed, monetary policy does matter.
The Reserve Bank of Australia kept its eye on inflation,
While our political leaders could sense our frustration.

So politicians pledged to increase our prosperity,
In a year full of promises made with sincerity.
But the dollar held firm as interest rates tumbled,
The economy improved but never quite rumbled.

Consumer spending was down and sentiment weak,
Retailers complained, the economy needs a tweak.
But the stimulus provided did not do the trick,
So we took the chance to give the government the flick.

With new political leadership, hopes are high,
That in the lead up to Christmas, Aussies will buy.
If the cash registers ring, all will be jolly,

Open your purses and merrily fill your trolley.

Now savers! Now borrowers! Now investors and spenders!
The economy needs a hero, you are all contenders.
While the rest of the world grapples with gloom and doom,
In the land of the Southern Cross, we are set to boom.

Our geographic location at the bottom of the Earth,
Means Christmas will be hot, from Penrith to Perth.
Across our wide brown land, summer will be amazing,
But we hope and pray no bushfires will be blazing.

For us a white Christmas is just a childhood dream,
Like sugar-plum fairies with peaches and cream.
But a visit from St Nicholas is on the cards,
Before you know it, he'll be landing in Aussie backyards.

So look up to the sky and you'll soon hear a thunder,
Santa's sleigh will be rockin', he's comin' Down Under.
He'll have lots of presents plus the gift of goodwill,
Let's embrace it warmly, it's not a bitter pill.

As I sign off for Christmas I thank each and every member,
It's been a pleasure to serve you, right through to December.
May the joy of the season fill your home on Christmas Day,
As we smile and gently whisper "Merry Christmas" from Gateway.

Posting Date: 16 December 2013

christmas 2014

'Tis the week before Christmas and on
my keyboard I'm pounding,
To compose a festive parody that's not trite sounding.
Everything is stirring, particularly my computer mouse,
Need to type faster, so I can go home to my house.

But as I sit at my desk looking squarely at my screen,
The lights are flashing, but not red, white and green.
This lack of colour does not dampen my spirits,
However, writing my seventh parody may test my limits.

So here we go again, let's see what's in my head,
After stretching my cranium, I'll shortly be snug in bed.
But for now the question is where to begin,
"I've got the answer," he says with a grin.

During the past year the home loan market did clatter,
Rising above the din, property prices were the chatter.
Auctions clearance rates were high,
reflecting pent-up demand,
It was good news for sellers, top prices they did command.

Across the nation, Australians watched their wealth rise,
Property ownership delivered us an envious prize.
The average Aussie is now worth more
than citizens elsewhere,
We are the richest people in the world,
with many a millionaire.

As a prosperous and generous people, we hosted the G20,
We were convivial hosts, with koala cuddling aplenty.
It was the largest gathering of world leaders to our nation,
As each stood at the lectern, we heard some great oration.

Now Barack! Now Vladimir! Now Shinzo and Angela,
You've got big jobs and we admire your stamina.
But words alone won't solve a single problem,
Concerted action is needed from Haiti to Harlem.

Here in Australia we have every reason to rejoice,
Our economy is growing and we have freedom of choice.
In a world of uncertainty, we live in a great place,
With safety and security and wide open space.

Sure we're not perfect and our dollar is too strong,
But unemployment is low, we should break into song.
Productivity remains an issue, we need more out of less,
"We know we can do better," the workers confess.

At this time of year it's appropriate to pause,
For the gifts we have, not including those from Santa Claus.
Our true wealth is not made up of material chattels,
It's who we are and overcoming our personal battles.

For now our thoughts turn to family and friends,
'Tis the season of goodwill, it's sad when it ends.
Yuletide celebrations bring out the best in us all,
Singing and laughing as we deck the hall.

As I sign off for Christmas I thank each and every member,
It's been a pleasure to serve you, right through to December.
May the joy of the season fill your home on Christmas Day,
As we smile and gently whisper "Merry Christmas" from Gateway.

Posting Date: 19 December 2014

christmas 2015

'Tis the week before Christmas in 2015,
And the man in the red suit is yet to be seen.
The stockings are hung in anticipation of his visit,
Singing and laughter, such joy does he elicit.

Australians are busy, not snug in their beds,
With last minute shopping and lists in their heads.
They rush to the stores for the latest apps,
More gadgets to buy, no time for naps.

With bags full of goodies, they make such a clatter,
There are bargains galore, so what I spend doesn't matter.
Retail sales are faltering, I must do my bit,
My fiscal stimulus should make the economy fit.

On the other side of the world, things are not so rosy,
Unlike Australia, the world's hotspots are not cozy.
Death and destruction caused by war and famine,
Living conditions are basic, no riches and mammon.

In this season of goodwill, we should reflect earnestly,
What our lives would be like if displaced undeservedly.
The plight of refugees touches all with a heart,
Millions looking for a home and seeking a fresh start.

Meanwhile, the rest of the world gets on with life,
In suburbs and towns there's relatively little strife.
Shopping online, double clicking their mouses,
Families order presents to fill their houses.

For the people of Greece it's been a difficult year,
Their sovereign debt crisis brought much fear.
Austerity measures demanded by international creditors,
Were seen by the people as bailouts by predators.

Across the seas at the US Federal Reserve,
Policymakers pondered what interest rates we deserve.
After much speculation about when to raise,
December's decision to increase was greeted with praise.

Back home in Oz, we watched the Rugby World Cup final,
The New Zealand All Blacks were a formidable rival.
The efforts of our Wallabies made us shout loud,
They didn't win, but still made us proud.

Gateway too had reason to cheer,
For the year just gone was our 60th year.
Our diamond birthday was a time to reflect,
On all that we've done, to earn our members' respect.

Now battle-droids! Now storm-troopers and bounty-hunters!
This Christmas sees the return of Star Wars for the punters.
Princess Leia, Han Solo, Luke Skywalker and Darth Vader,
The original cast is back, battling another invader.

But for now our thoughts turn to the season of goodwill,
And the excitement that comes from stockings to fill.
It won't be long before Santa's on his way,
If you listen carefully, you'll soon hear his sleigh.

As I sign off for Christmas I thank each and every member,
It's been a pleasure to serve you, right through to December.
May the joy of the season fill your home on Christmas Day,
As we smile and gently whisper "Merry Christmas" from Gateway.

Posting Date: 21 December 2015

Afterword

Please allow me to begin this ending with an adage from legendary English writer, Samuel Johnson: "A writer only begins a book. A reader finishes it." Thank you for getting to the end of this book. Dr Johnson also said that "the two engaging powers of an author are to make new things familiar and familiar things new". I hope I have done just that.

The tale of how *Bite Size Advice* came to be can be traced back to late 2007. At that stage, Gateway Credit Union was redesigning its website and my then Head of Marketing, Loyce Cox-Paton, informed me that the new site would have provision for a CEO blog. My immediate response was to ask - what's a blog?

I was told that a blog is a form of self-publishing which enables you to share your thoughts and ideas with people online via a publicly accessible journal. After I digested what that meant I said: "Thanks, but no thanks." But Loyce persisted and I reluctantly agreed to start blogging. My first blog post was published on 25 March 2008 and is reproduced here:

> I must confess to feeling a tad nervous. I'd never heard of a blog 12 months ago. Yet here I am today sharing

my thoughts publicly. I've always considered myself a frustrated writer, so I'm happy to accede to the wishes of my executive colleagues and give blogging a go.

I've had a crash course in blogging and think I understand the rules of the game. It's been drilled into me that CEO blogs are not for corporate spin but for honest opinions. My aim is to write my blogs in a conversational style to facilitate open, two-way communication.

The danger that all leaders face is receiving only filtered feedback. With the best of intentions, sometimes the bad news does not get to the CEO. Of course, the real boss in any organisation is the customer and I'm keen to hear from our members and potential members.

So, please use this new communication medium to tell me what you think. I have broad shoulders, so you can be frank. If we've made a mistake or fallen short in our service delivery, I'll unreservedly apologise. However, I'll draw the line at feedback which is unnecessarily rude or profane.

Well, I have never received offensive feedback on my blog and my readership continues to grow. A new reader to my blog about three years ago was Katherine Owen. Katherine and I met a short time earlier at an industry event and following that she subscribed to my blog.

I caught up with Katherine in the latter part of 2014 and she serendipitously informed me that she had started her own publishing company. Harbouring a life-long desire to publish, I seized the opportunity and asked Katherine if she would consider publishing the blog in book format and to my delight she agreed.

The first step in the blog to book process was obtaining

AFTERWORD

the approval of my board of directors. My blog is not a personal blog but a corporate blog, written by me in my capacity as CEO of Gateway Credit Union. I thank the board for approving my request and acknowledge each of my directors viz, Catherine Hallinan, John Flynn, Steve Carritt, Mal Graham, Graham Raward and Rene van der Loos.

Little did I know that the next step on the road to publishing would be so difficult. Katherine told me that the ideal word count for my book was 50,000 to 60,000 words. That meant I had to cull about 200 of the 300 blog posts I had written. The culling process straddled a three week period and occurred in three stages. At the end of the third cull, I was within Katherine's word count limit.

My final challenge was to sort the remaining 100 posts into common themes so that they could form chapters. My first two attempts at sorting the blogs into subject categories proved futile. Then, after a week of quiet reflection and contemplation (to keep a lid on my frustration!), the answer hit me - sort the blog posts using a PEST framework.

For the uninitiated, a PEST analysis is a simple and widely used tool that helps a business to evaluate the impact that Political, Economic, Social and Technological issues may have on its operations. To my delight, I found that the blog posts could be categorised into one of the four PEST areas and these became the thematic book chapters.

I continue to blog and publish a new post every Monday morning (Sydney time). Those readers wishing to follow my blog and receive the latest blog content can do so using the RSS subscription button at www.gatewaycu.com.au/CEOBlog

Resource List

This resource list acknowledges my debt to the many and varied sources of data and ideas I drew upon in researching and writing the 100 blog posts contained in this book. The list is arranged under the medium of publication and each citation includes sufficient information - including a URL where appropriate - to allow that source to be located and retrieved.

PUBLISHED BOOKS

Attali, Jacques. 2009. *A Brief History Of The Future*. Sydney: Allen & Unwin.

Bogan, David and Davies, Keith. 2007. *Avoid retirement and stay alive: Why you should never retire and how not to*. Sydney: Harper Collins Publishers.

Carr, Nicholas. 2009. *The Big Switch: Rewiring The World, From Edison To Google*. New York: W.W. Norton & Company.

Chang, Ha-Joon. 2011. *23 Things They Don't Tell You About Capitalism*. London: Penguin Books.

Davies, Paul. 2002. *How To Build A Time Machine*. Melbourne: Penguin Books.

Ehrlich, Paul R. 1968. *The Population Explosion*. New York: Buccaneer Books.

Ferguson, Niall. 2008. *The Ascent Of Money: A Financial History Of The World*. Melbourne: Penguin Group (Australia).

Gladwell, Malcolm. 2011. *Outliers: The story of success*. New York: Back Bay Books.

Gleick, James. 1988. *Chaos: Making a New Science*. London: Vintage Books (Random House).

Honoré, Carl. 2005. *In Praise of Slow: How A Worldwide Movement is Challenging The Cult Of Speed*. London: Orion Books.

Mahbubani, Kishore. 2009. *The New Asian Hemisphere: The Irresistible Shift Of Global Power To The East*. New York: Public Affairs™.

Moody, James Bradfield and Nogrady, Bianca. 2010. *The Sixth Wave: How to succeed in a resource-limited world*. Sydney: Vintage Books (Random House).

Safire, William (ed). 1997. *Lend Me Your Ears: Great Speeches In History*. Revised and expanded edn. New York: W.W. Norton & Company.

Shiller, Robert J. 2005. *Irrational Exuberance*. 2nd edn. Princeton, NJ: Princeton University Press.

Shiller, Robert J. 2012. *Finance and the Good Society*. Princeton, NJ: Princeton University Press.

Simon, Phil. 2013. *The Age of the Platform: How Amazon,

Apple, Facebook, and Google Have Redefined Business. Revised edn. Henderson, Nevada: Motion Publishing.

Syed, Matthew. 2011. *Bounce: The myth of talent and the power of practice*. London: Fourth Estate.

The Economist. 2015. *Pocket World in Figures*. 2015 edn. London: Economists Books.

NEWSPAPER ARTICLES

Aly, Waleed. 2008. 'Beneath the financial crisis waits a nastier beast'. *The Sydney Morning Herald* (online). 13 October. Available: www.smh.com.au/news/opinion/the-markets-will-stabilise-but-then-what-happens/2008/10/12/1223749846530.html?

Appelbaum, Binyamin. 2014. 'Does Hosting the Olympics Actually Pay Off?'. *The New York Times Magazine* (online). 5 August. Available: http://www.nytimes.com/2014/08/10/magazine/does-hosting-the-olympics-actually-pay-off.html?_r=2

Benson, Simon. 2015. 'There is an obvious inequity in our tax system ... and it is unsustainable'. *The Daily Telegraph* (online). 27 February. Available: www.dailytelegraph.com.au/news/opinion/there-is-an-obvious-inequity-in-our-tax-system-and-it-is-unsustainable/story-fni0cwl5-1227240417751

Bishop, Julie. 2010. 'Vote - or else?'. *The Age* (online). 3 March. Available: http://www.theage.com.au/it-pro/vote--or-else-20100302-pgqd.html

Cowie, Tom. 2014. 'Too few brickies for the walls'. *The Sydney Morning Herald* (online). 11 June. Available:

www.smh.com.au/business/too-few-brickies-for-the-walls-20140610-39vk6.html

de Brito, Sam. 2014. 'The singular problem facing mankind'. *The Sydney Morning Herald* (online). 9 November. Available: www.smh.com.au/comment/the-singular-problem-facing-mankind-20141101-11fhvh

Feneley, Rick and Hutchens, Gareth. 2014. 'Hard times ahead for Generation Less'. *The Sydney Morning Herald* (online). 13 December. Available: www.smh.com.au/business/the-economy/hard-times-ahead-for-generation-less-20141212-125re4.html

Gray, Sadie. 2008. 'Archbishops attack profiteers and "bank robbers" in City'. *The Guardian* (online). 25 September. Available: http://www.theguardian.com/world/2008/sep/25/religion.creditcrunch

Horin, Adele. 2010. 'Bigger Australia as certain as death and taxes'. *The Sydney Morning Herald* (online). 7 October. Available: http://www.smh.com.au/national/bigger-australia-as-certain-as-death-and-taxes-20101006-167w1.html

Kassam, Ashifa and Scammell, Roise. 2015. 'Europe needs many more babies to avert a population disaster'. *The Guardian* (online). 23 August. Available: www.theguardian.com/world/2015/aug/23/baby-crisis-europe-brink-depopulation-disaster

Lunn, Stephen and Hepworth, Annabel. 2010. 'Reject little Australia: PM Advisers'. *The Australian* (online). 22 July. Available: www.theaustralian.com.au/national-affairs/reject-little-australia-pm-advisers/story-fn59niix-1225895329058

Martin, Peter. 2015. 'Low 10-year bond rates are the deal of the century but Abbott's not at the table'. *The Age* (online). 21 January. Available: www.theage.com.au/comment/low-10year-bond-rates-are-the-deal-of-the-century-but-abbotts-not-at-the-table-20150119-12tq4j

Patty, Anna. 2014. 'Graduate glut puts trainee teachers on the scrapheap'. *The Sydney Morning Herald* (online). 20 October. Available: www.smh.com.au/national/education/graduate-glut-puts-trainee-teachers-on-the-scrapheap-20141019-115wa4.html

Peatling, Stephanie. 2009. 'Populate and perish'. *The Sydney Morning Herald* (online). 15 November. Available: http://www.smh.com.au/federal-politics/political-opinion/populate-and-perish-20091114-ifxx

Rayner, Gordon. 2008. 'Global financial crisis: does the world need a new banking policeman?'. *The Telegraph* (online). 7 October. Available: http://www.telegraph.co.uk/finance/comment/3155122/Global-financial-crisis-does-the-world-need-a-new-banking-policeman.html

Rogoff, Kenneth. 2014. 'Paper money is unfit for a world of high crime and low inflation'. *Financial Times* (online). 28 May. Available: http://www.ft.com/cms/s/0/c47c87ae-e284-11e3-a829-00144feabdc0.html#axzz3zvE9w8j2

Russell, Helen. 2014. 'Welcome to Sweden - the most cash-free society on the planet'. *The Guardian* (online). 12 November. Available: http://www.theguardian.com/world/2014/nov/11/welcome-sweden-electronic-money-not-so-funny

Salt, Bernard. 2015. 'Inconvenient truth on tax a bit rich'. *The Australian*. 26 February.

Schwarz, Hunter. 2015. 'Proof that voter turnout in the U.S. is embarrassing'. *The Washington Post* (online). 6 May. Available: https://www.

washingtonpost.com/news/the-fix/wp/2015/05/06/proof-that-voter-turnout-in-the-u-s-is-embarrassing/

Smith, Alexandra. 2015. 'Education in NSW: Calls for overhaul of high school because of university entry focus'. *The Sydney Morning Herald* (online). 19 February. Available: www.smh.com.au/nsw/education-in-nsw-calls-for-overhaul-of-high-school-because-of-university-entry-focus-20150218-13ivt2

Vanstone, Amanda. 2014. 'Rich versus poor is the wrong debate'. *The Sydney Morning Herald* (online). 13 October. Available: www.smh.com.au/comment/rich-versus-poor-is-the-wrong-debate-20141010-114era

Zappone, Chris. 2009. 'Jobless fears hit home'. *The Sydney Morning Herald* (online). 14 July. Available: http://www.smh.com.au/business/jobless-fears-hit-home-20090714-djco.html

Zimbalist, Andrew. 2012. '3 Reasons Why Hosting The Olympics Is a Loser's Game'. *The Atlantic* (online). 23 July. Available: http://www.theatlantic.com/business/archive/2012/07/3-reasons-why-hosting-the-olympics-is-a-losers-game/260111/

MAGAZINES & PERIODICALS

Bonchek Mark and Choudary, Sangeet Paul. 2013. 'Three Elements of a Successful Platform Strategy'. *Harvard Business Review* (online). 31 January. Available: https://hbr.org/2013/01/three-elements-of-a-successful-platform

Libert, Barry., Wind, Yoram (Jerry) and Fenley, Megan Beck. 2014. 'What Airbnb, Uber, and Alibaba Have in Common'. *Harvard Business Review* (online).

20 November. Available: https://hbr.org/2014/11/what-airbnb-uber-and-alibaba-have-in-common

Matthews, Chris. 2015. 'This country wants to ban the use of cash in stores'. *Fortune* (online). 22 May. Available: http://fortune.com/2015/05/22/denmark-paper-money/

Sivy, Michael. 2012. 'Where the Fed's Profits Come From'. *Time* (online). 26 March. Available: http://business.time.com/2012/03/26/where-the-feds-profits-come-from/

'The other side of QE: What happens when the fed starts losing money'. *The Economist* (online). 26 January 2013. Available: http://www.economist.com/news/finance-and-economics/21570753-what-happens-when-fed-starts-losing-money-other-side-qe

MEDIA OUTLETS

Berg, Chris. 2013. 'Foreign investment is always a two-faced policy'. *The Drum* (online). 18 September. Available: http://www.abc.net.au/news/2013-09-17/berg-foreign-investment-abbott-government/4962416

Corden, Max. 2014. 'Australia needs higher taxes, not spending cuts'. *The Conversation* (online). 5 December. Available: http://theconversation.com/australia-needs-higher-taxes-not-spending-cuts-34657

Dean, Tim. 2014. 'Cheer up, it's not all doom and gloom'. *The Drum* (online). 16 October. Available: http://www.abc.net.au/news/2014-10-16/dean-cheer-up,-it's-not-all-doom-and-gloom/5818302

Freebairn, John. 2012. 'Australia's productivity problem: why it matters'. *The Conversation* (online).

2 August. Available: http://theconversation.com/australias-productivity-problem-why-it-matters-8584

Garnett, Anne. 2013. 'Why not let agriculture benefit from foreign investment?'. *The Conversation* (online). 4 November. Available: www.theconversation.com/why-not-let-agriculture-benefit-from-foreign-investment-19433

Graham, Fiona. 2013. 'Wearable technology: The bra designed to shock attackers'. *BBC News* (online). 16 April. Available: http://www.bbc.com/news/business-22110443

Janda, Michael. 2012. 'Australian homes still among least affordable'. *ABC News* (online). Available: http://www.abc.net.au/news/2012-01-23/australia-housing-affordability-twt/3788114

Madden, John and Giesecke, James. 2012. 'Hosting the Olympics: cash cow or money pit?'. *The Conversation* (online). 26 July. Available: http://theconversation.com/hosting-the-olympics-cash-cow-or-money-pit-7403

Manning, Paddy. 2013. 'The problem with debt is that we don't have enough of it'. *Crikey* (online). 15 November. Available: http://www.crikey.com.au/2013/11/15/the-problem-with-debt-is-we-dont-have-enough-of-it/

Melik, Mark. 2009. 'The dangers of trade protectionism'. *BBC World Service* (online). 4 February. Available: http://news.bbc.co.uk/2/hi/business/7866930.stm

Millane, Emily. 2014. 'Class, not generation, is the real dividing line'. *The Drum* (online). 18 December. Available: www.abc.net.au/news/2014-12-18/millane-class,-not-generation,-is-the-real-dividing-line/5971016

Verrender, Ian. 2014. 'Don't worry: Australia was

built on foreign investment'. *The Drum* (online). 24 November. Available: http://www.abc.net.au/news/2014-11-24/verrender-australia-was-built-on-foreign-investment/5913224

Walker, Andrew. 2016. 'Why use negative interest rates?'. *BBC World Service* (Online). 15 February. Available: http://www.bbc.com/news/business-32284393

DIGITAL NEWS SITES

Jackson, Allison. 2016. 'What it means when interest rates fall below zero percent'. *GlobalPost* (online). 13 February. Available: http://www.globalpost.com/article/6732009/2016/02/11/more-central-banks-are-loving-negative-interest-rates-right-now

O'Grady, Sean. 2008. 'The butterfly effect: How a blip became a credit crunch'. *Independent* (online). 7 August. Available: http://www.independent.co.uk/money/spend-save/the-butterfly-effect-how-a-blip-became-a-credit-crunch-887059.html

Scutt, David. 2016. 'There's a big problem with the last tool in the arsenal of the world's central banks'. *Business Insider Australia* (online). 17 February. Available: http://www.businessinsider.com/theres-a-big-problem-with-negative-interest-rates-2016-2?IR=T

BUSINESS PUBLICATIONS

Deloitte Touche Tohmatsu Limited. 2014. 'Digital disruption: Threats and opportunities for retail financial services'. April. Available: www2.deloitte.com/global/en/pages/financial-services/articles/digital-disruption-in-fsi.html

KPMG. 2014. 'The 50 Best Fintech Innovators Report'. December. Available: www.kpmg.com/AU/en/IssuesAndInsights/ArticlesPublications/Documents/50-best-fintech-innovators-report-2014.pdf

GOVERNMENT PUBLICATIONS

Australian Government, Treasury. 2010. *Intergenerational Report 2010: Australia to 2050: Future challenges*. 1 February. Available: archive.treasury.gov.au/igr/igr2010/report/pdf/IGR_2010.pdf

Australian Workforce and Productivity Agency, Discussion Paper, 2012. *Australia's skills and workforce development needs*. July. Available: docs.education.gov.au/system/files/doc/other/future-focus-australias-skills-and-workforce-development-needs-discussion-paper-2012.pdf

McLeay, Michael., Radia, Amar and Thomas, Ryland. 2014. 'Money in the modern economy: an introduction'. *Bank of England, Quarterly Bulletin*, 2014 Q1 (online). Available: www.bankofengland.co.uk/publications/Documents/quarterlybulletin/2014/qb14q101.pdf

The Reserve Bank of Australia. 1997. '*Measuring profits from currency issue*'. July. Available: http://www.rba.gov.au/publications/bulletin/1997/jul/pdf/bu-0797-1.pdf

RESEARCH REPORTS

Daley, John and Wood, Danielle. 2014. 'The wealth of generations'. *Grattan Institute*. December. Available: www.grattan.edu.au/wp-content/uploads/2014/12/820-wealth-of-generations3.pdf

Ericsson, K, Anders., Krampe, Ralf and Tesch-Römer, Clemens. 1993. 'The role of deliberate practice in the acquisition of expert performance'. *Psychological Review*, Vol. 100, No. 3, 363-406. Available: www.projects.ict.usc.edu/itw/gel/EricssonDeliberatePracticePR93.pdf

Foundation for Young Australians. 2015. 'The New Work Order: Ensuring young Australians have skills and experience for the jobs of the future, not the past'. November. Available: www.fya.org.au/wp-content/uploads/2015/08/fya-future-of-work-report-final-lr.pdf

Zhang, Bohui. 2013. 'Companies Under Attack: Should Short Sellers Be Encouraged or Reigned In'. *BusinessThink*. UNSW Australian Business School (online). 11 November. Available: www.businessthink.unsw.edu.au/Pages/Companies-Under-Attack--Should-Short-Sellers-Be-Encouraged-or-Reined-In.aspx

THINK TANKS

Baily, Martin Neil and Elliott, Douglas J. 2013. 'The Role of Finance in the Economy: Implications for Structural Reform of the Financial Sector'. *The Brookings Institution* (online). 11 July. Available: www.brookings.edu/~/media/research/files/papers/2013/07/11-finance-role-in-economy-baily-elliott/11-finance-role-in-economy-baily-elliott.pdf

SPEECHES

Brogden, John. 2013. '2013 - the Election and Financial Services'. Speech delivered to FSC Deloitte Leadership

Series Lunch. 21 February. Available: http://www.fsc.org.au/downloads/file/MediaReleaseFile/2013_0221FSCSpeech-theElectionandFinancialServices.pdf

WEBSITES

Chamie, Joseph. 2015. 'Humanity's Future: Below Replacement Fertility?'. *Global Issues* (website). 15 January. Available: http://www.globalissues.org/news/2015/01/15/20508

About the Author

Paul Thomas has worked in the financial services industry for 40 years. His journey from bank teller to credit union CEO began in 1976. He followed an old-fashioned career path that saw him rise through the ranks. Along the way, he gained broad experience in retail banking across a range of financial institutions.

Versed in all aspects of management, Paul is a high calibre executive with particular expertise in strategy development and execution. His deep knowledge of contemporary issues coupled with his passion for communication find expression in his weekly blog. He writes respectfully and insightfully - but without fear or favour - for the public at large.

Paul has developed a reputation as a thought leader and commentator on the contemporary political, economic, social and technological issues facing business and society. He offers informed insights and opinions in an authoritative voice that is authentic and engaging.

An accomplished public speaker and writer, Paul's credentials include an MBA and a Diploma in Financial Services.

www.ingramcontent.com/pod-product-compliance
Lightning Source LLC
LaVergne TN
LVHW021653060526
838200LV00050B/2326